NATIONAL SYSTEM OF
POLITICAL ECONOMY
VOLUME 1: THE HISTORY

NATIONAL SYSTEM OF POLITICAL ECONOMY

VOLUME 1: THE HISTORY

FRIEDRICH LIST

COSMO CLASSICS

NEW YORK

National System of Political Economy
Volume 1: The History
Cover © 2005 by Cosimo, Inc.

National System of Political Economy, Volume 1: The History
was originally published in 1841.

For information, address:
P.O. Box 416, Old Chelsea Station
New York, NY 10011

or visit our website at:
www.cosimobooks.com

Ordering Information:
Cosimo publications are available at online bookstores. They may
also be purchased for educational, business or promotional use:
- *Bulk orders:* special discounts are available on bulk orders for reading
groups, organizations, businesses, and others. For details contact
Cosimo Special Sales at the address above or at info@cosimobooks.com.
- *Custom-label orders:* we can prepare selected books with your cover or
logo of choice. For more information, please contact Cosimo at
info@cosimobooks.com.

ISBN: 1-596-05542-1

Chapter 1

The Italians

At the revival of civilisation in Europe, no county was in so favourable a position as Italy in respect to commerce and industry. Barbarism had not been able entirely to eradicate the culture and civilisation of ancient Rome. A genial climate and a fertile soil, notwithstanding an unskilful system of cultivation, yielded abundant nourishment for a numerous population. The most necessary arts and industries remained as little destroyed as the municipal institutions of ancient Rome. Prosperous coast fisheries served everywhere as nurseries for seamen, and navigation along Italy's extensive sea-coasts abundantly compensated her lack of internal means of transport. Her proximity to Greece, Asia Minor, and Egypt, and her maritime intercourse with them, secured for Italy special advantages in the trade with the East which had previously, though not extensively, been carried on through Russia with the countries of the North. By means of this commercial intercourse Italy necessarily acquired those branches of knowledge and those arts and manufactures which Greece had preserved from the civilisation of ancient times.

From the period of the emancipation of the Italian cities by Otho the Great, they gave evidence of what history was testified alike in earlier and later times, namely, that freedom and industry are inseparable companions, even although not unfrequently the one has come into existence before the other. If commerce and industry are flourishing anywhere, one may be certain that there freedom is nigh at hand: if anywhere Freedom was unfolded her banner, it is as certain that sooner or later industry will there establish herself; for nothing is more natural than that when man has acquired material or mental wealth he should strive to obtain guarantees for the transmission of his acquisitions to his successors, or that when he has acquired freedom, he should devote all his energies to improve his physical and intellectual condition.

For the first time since the downfall of the free states of antiquity was the spectacle again presented to the world by the cities of Italy of free and rich communities. Cities and territories reciprocally rose to a state of prosperity and received a powerful impulse in that direction from the Crusades. The transport of the Crusaders and their baggage and material of war not only benefited Italy's navigation, it afforded also inducements and opportunities for the conclusion of advantageous commercial relations with the East for the introduction of new industries, inventions, and plants, and for acquaintance with new enjoyments. On the other hand, the oppressions of feudal lordship were weakened and diminished in manifold ways, owing to the same cause, tending to the greater freedom of the cities and of the cultivation of the soil.

Next after Venice and Genoa, Florence became especially conspicuous for her manufactures and her monetary exchange business. Already, in the twelfth and thirteenth centuries, her silk and woollen manufactures were very flourishing; the guilds of those trades took part in the government, and under their influence the Republic was constituted. The woollen manufacture alone employed 200 manufactories, which produced annually 80,000 pieces of cloth, the raw material for which was imported from Spain. In addition to these, raw cloth to the amount of 300,000 gold gulden was imported annually from Spain, France, Belgium, and Germany, which, after being finished at Florence, was exported to the Levant. Florence conducted the banking business of the whole of Italy, and contained eighty banking establishments.(1*) The annual revenue of her Government amounted to 300,000 gold gulden (fifteen million francs of our present money), considerably more than the revenue of the kingdoms of Naples and Aragon at that period, and more than that of Great Britain and Ireland under Queen Elizabeth.(2*)

We thus see Italy in the twelfth and thirteenth centuries possessing all the elements of national economical prosperity, and in respect of both commerce and industry far in advance of all other nations. Her agriculture and her manufactures served as patterns and as motives for emulation to other countries. Her roads and canals were the best in Europe. The civilised world is indebted to her for banking institutions, the mariner's compass, improved naval architecture, the system of exchanges, and a host of the most useful commercial customs and commercial laws, as well as for a great part of its municipal and govern-mental institutions. Her commercial, marine, and naval power were by far the most important in the southern seas. She was in possession of the trade of the world; for, with the exception of the unimportant portion of it carried on over the northern seas, that trade was confined to the Mediterranean and the Black Sea. She supplied all nations with manufactures, with articles of luxury, and with tropical products, and was supplied by them with raw materials. One thing alone was wanting to Italy to enable her to become what England has become in our days, and because that one thing was wanting to her, every other element of prosperity passed away from her; she lacked na-tional union and the power which springs from it. The cities and ruling powers of Italy did not act as members of one body, but made war on and ravaged one another like independent

9

powers and states. While these wars raged externally, each commonwealth was successively overthrown by the internal conflicts between democracy, aristocracy, and autocracy. These conflicts, so destructive to national prosperity, were stimulated and increased by foreign powers and their invasions, and by the power of the priesthood at home and its pernicious influence, whereby the separate Italian communities were arrayed against one another in two hostile factions.

How Italy thus destroyed herself may be best learned from the history of her maritime states. We first see Amalfi great and powerful (from the eighth to the eleventh century).(3*) Her ships covered the seas, and all the coin which passed current in Italy and the Levant was that of Amalfi. She possessed the most practical code of maritime laws, and those laws were in force in every port of the Mediterranean. In the twelfth century her naval power was destroyed by Pisa, Pisa in her turn fell under the attacks of Genoa, and Genoa herself, after a conflict of a hundred years, was compelled to succumb to Venice.

The fall of Venice herself appears to have indirectly resulted from this narrow-minded policy. To a league of Italian naval powers it could not have been a difficult task, not merely to maintain and uphold the preponderance of Italy in Greece, Asia Minor, the Archipelago, and Egypt, but continually to extend and strengthen it; or to curb the progress of the Turks on land and repress their piracies at sea, while contesting with the Portuguese the passage round the Cape of Good Hope.

As matters actually stood, however, Venice was not merely left to her own resources, she found herself crippled by the external attacks of her sister states and of the neighbonring European powers.

It could not have proved a difficult task to a well-organised league of Italian military powers to defend the independence of

Italy against the aggression of the great monarchies. The attempt to form such a league was actually made in 1526, but then not until the moment of actual danger and only for temporary defence. The lukewarmness and treachery of the leaders and members of this league were the cause of the subsequent subjugation of Milan and the fall of the Tuscan Republic. From that period must be dated the downfall of the industry and commerce of Italy.(4*)

In her earlier as well as in her later history Venice aimed at being a nation for herself alone. So long as she had to deal only with petty Italian powers or with decrepid Greece, she had no difficulty in maintaining a supremacy in manufactures and commerce through the countries bordering on the Mediterranean and Black Seas. As soon, however, as united and vigorous nations appeared on the political stage, it became manifest at once that Venice was merely a city and her aristocracy only a municipal one. It is true that she had conquered several islands and even extensive provinces, but she ruled over them only as conquered territory, and hence (according to the testimony of all historians) each conquest increased her weakness instead of her power

At the same period the spirit within the Republic by which she had grown great gradually died away. The power and prosperity of Venice — the work of a patriotic and heroic aristocracy which had sprung from an energetic and liberty-loving democracy-maintained itself and increased so long as the freedom of democratic energy lent it support, and that energy was guided by the patriotism, the wisdom, and the heroic spirit of the aristocracy. But in proportion as the aristocracy became a despotic oligarchy, destructive of the freedom and energies of the people, the roots of power and prosperity died away, notwithstanding that their branches and leading

11

stem appeared still to flourish for some time longer.'(5*)

A nation which has fallen into slavery,' says Montesquieu,(6*) 'strives rather to retain what it possesses than to acquire more; a free nation, on the contrary, strives rather to acquire than to retain.' To this very true observation he might have added — and because anyone strives only to retain without acquiring he must come to grief, for every nation which makes no forward progress sinks lower and lower, and must ultimately fall. Far from striving to extend their commerce and to make new discoveries, the Venetians never even conceived the idea of deriving benefit from the discoveries made by other nations. That they could be excluded from the trade with the East Indies by the discovery of the new commercial route thither, never occurred to them until they actually experienced it. What all the rest of the world perceived they would not believe; and when they began to find out the injurious results of the altered state of things, they strove to maintain the old commercial route instead of seeking to participate in the benefits of the new one; they endeavoured to maintain by petty intrigues what could only be won by making wise use of the altered circumstances by the spirit of enterprise and by hardihood. And when they at length had lost what they had possessed, and the wealth of the East and West indies was pouted into Cadiz and Lisbon instead of into their own ports, like simpletons or spendthrifts they turned their attention to alchemy.(7*)

In the times when the Republic grew and flourished, to be inscribed in the Golden Book was regarded as a reward for distinguished exertions in commerce, in industry, or in the civil or military service of the State. On that condition this honour was open to foreigners; for example, to the most distinguished of the silk manufacturers who had immigrated from Florence.(8*) But that book was closed when men began to regard places of honour and State salaries as the family inheritance of the patrician class. At a later period, when men recognised the necessity of giving new life to the impoverished and enfeebled aristocracy, the book was reopened. But the chief title to inscription in it was no longer, as in former times, to have rendered services to the State, but the possession of wealth and noble birth. At length the honour of being inscribed in the Golden Book was so little esteemed, that it remained open for a century with scarcely any additional names.

If we inquire of History what were the causes of the downfall of this Republic and of its commerce, she replies that they principally consisted in the folly, neglect, and cowardice of a worn-out aristocracy, and in the apathy of a people who had sunk into slavery. The commerce and manufactures of Venice must have declined, even if the new route round the Cape of Good Hope had never been discovered.

The cause of it, as of the fall of all the other Italian republics, is to be found in the absence of national unity, in the domination of foreign powers, in priestly rule at home, and in the rise of other greater, more powerful, and more united nationalities in Europe.

If we carefully consider the commercial policy of Venice, we see at a glance that that of modern commercial and manufacturing nations is but a copy of that of Venice, only on an enlarged (i.e. a national) scale. By navigation laws and customs duties in each case native vessels and native manufactures were protected against those of foreigners, and the maxim thus early held good that it was sound policy to import raw materials from other states and to export to them manufactured goods.(9*)

It has been recently asserted in defence of the principle of absolute and unconditional free trade, that her protective policy was the cause of the downfall of Venice. That assertion comprises a little truth with a great deal of error if we investigate the history of Venice with an unprejudiced eye, we find that in her case, as in that of the great kingdoms at a later period, freedom of international trade as well as restrictions on it have been beneficial or prejudicial to the power and prosperity of the State at different epochs. Unrestricted freedom of trade was beneficial to the Republic in the first years of her existence; for how otherwise could she have raised herself from a mere fishing village to a commercial power? But a protective policy was also beneficial to her when she had arrived at a certain stage of power and wealth, for by means of it she attained to manufacturing and commercial supremacy. Protection first became injurious to her when her manufacturing and commercial power had reached that supremacy, because by it all competition with other nations became absolutely excluded, and thus indolence was encouraged. Therefore, not the introduction of a protective policy, but perseverance in maintaining it after the reasons for its introduction had passed away, was really injurious to Venice.

Hence the argument to which we have adverted has this great fault, that it takes no account of the rise of great nations under hereditary monarchy. Venice, although mistress of some provinces and islands, yet being all the time merely one Italian city, stood in competition, at the period of her rise to a manufacturing and commercial power, merely with other Italian cities; and her prohibitory commercial policy could benefit her so long only as whole nations with united power did not enter into competition with her. But as soon as that took place, she could only have maintained her supremacy by placing herself at the head of a united Italy and by embracing in her commercial system the whole Italian nation. No commercial policy was ever clever enough to maintain continuously the commercial supremacy of a single city over united nations.

From the example of Venice (so far as it may be adduced against a protective commercial policy at the present time) neither more nor less can be inferred than this — that a single city or a small state cannot establish and maintain such a policy successfully in competition with great states and kingdoms; also that any power which by means of a protective policy has attained a position of manufacturing and commercial supremacy, can (after she has attained it) revert with advantage to the policy of free trade.

In the argument before adverted to, as in every other when international freedom of trade is the subject of discussion, we meet with a misconception which has been the parent of much error, occasioned by the misuse of the term 'freedom.' Freedom of trade is spoken of in the same terms as religious freedom and municipal freedom. Hence the friends and advocates of freedom feel themselves especially bound to defend freedom in all its forms. And thus the term 'free trade' has become popular without drawing the necessary distinction between freedom of internal trade within the State and freedom of trade between separate nations, notwithstanding that these two in their nature and operation are as distinct as the heaven is from the earth. For while restrictions on the internal trade of a state are compatible in only very few cases with the liberty of individual citizens, in the case of international trade the highest degree of individual liberty may consist with a high degree of protective policy. Indeed, it is even possible that the greatest freedom of international trade may result in national servitude, as we hope hereafter to show from the case of Poland. In respect to this Montesquieu says truly, 'Commerce is never subjected to greater restrictions than in free nations, and never subjected to less ones than in those under despotic government.'(10*)

NOTES:

1. De l'Ecluse, Florence et ses Vicissitudes, pp. 23, 26, 32, 163, 213.

2. Pechio, Histoire de l'Economie Politique en Italie.

3. Amalfi contained at the period of her prosperity 50,000 inhabitants. Flavio Guio, the inventor of the mariner's compass, was a citizen of Amalfi. It was the sack of Amalfi by the Pisans (1135 or 1137) that that ancient book was discovered which later on became so injurious to the freedom and energies of Germany — the Pandects.

4. Hence Charles V was the destroyer of commerce and industry in Italy, as he was also in the Netherlands and in Spain. He was the introducer of nobility by patent, and of the idea that it was disgraceful for the nobility to carry on commerce or manufactures — an idea which had the most destructive influence on the national industry. Before his time the contrary idea prevailed; the Medici continued to be engaged in commerce long after they had become sovereign rulers.

5. "Quand les nobles, au lien de verser leur sang pour la patrie, au lieu d'illustrer l'etat par des victoires et de l'agrandir par des conquetes, n'eurent plus qu'a jouir des honneurs et a se partager des impots on dut se demander pourquoi il y avait huit ou neuf cents habitants de Venice qui se disaient proprietaries de toute la Republique." (Daru, Histoire de Venise, vol. iv. ch. xviii.)

6. Esprit des Lois, p. 192.

7. A mere charlatan, Marco Brasadino, who professed to have the art of making gold, was welcomed by the Venetian aristocracy as a saviour. (Daru, Histoire de Venise, vol. iii. ch. xix.)

8. Venice, as Holland and England subsequently did, made use of every opportunity of attracting to herself manufacturing industry and capital from foreign states. Also a considerable number of silk manufacturers emigrated to Venice from Luces, where already in the thirteenth century the manufacturer of velvets and brocades was very flourishing, in consequence of the oppression of the Lucchese tyrant Castruccio Castracani. (Sandu, Histoire de Venise, vol. i. pp. 247-256.)

9. Sismondi, Histoire des Republiques Italiennes, Pt. I, p. 285.

10. Esprit des Lois, livre xx. ch. xii.

Chapter 2

The Hansards

The spirit of industry, commerce, and liberty having attained full influence in Italy, crossed the Alps, permeated Germany, and erected for itself a new throne on the shores of the northern seas, the Emperor Henry I, the father of the liberator of the Italian municipalities, promoted the founding of new cities and the enlargement of older ones which were already partly established on the sites of the ancient Roman colonies and partly in the imperial domains.

Like the kings of France and England at a later period, he and his successors regarded the cities as the strongest counterpoise to the aristocracy, as the richest source of revenue to the State, as a new basis for national defence. By means of their commercial relations with the cities of Italy, their competition with Italian industry, and their free institutions, these cities soon attained to a high degree of prosperity and civilisation. Life in common fellow-citizenship created a spirit of progress in the arts and in manufacture, as well as zeal to achieve distinction by wealth and by enterprise; while, on the other hand, the acquisition of material wealth stimulated exertions to acquire culture and improvement in their political condition.

Strong through the power of youthful freedom and of flourishing industry, but exposed to the attacks of robbers by land and sea, the maritime towns of Northern Germany soon felt the necessity of a closer mutual union for protection and defence. With this object Hamburg and Lübeck formed a league in 1241, which before the close of that century embraced all the cities of any importance on the coasts of the Baltic and North Seas, or on the banks of the Oder, the Elbe, the Weser, and the Rhine (eighty-five in all). This confederation adopted the title of the 'Hansa,' which in the Low German dialect signifies a league.

Promptly comprehending what advantages the industry of individuals might derive from a union of their forces, the Hansa lost no time in developing and establishing a commercial policy which resulted in a degree of commercial prosperity previously unexampled. Perceiving that whatever power desires to create and maintain an extensive maritime commerce, must possess the means of defending it, they created a powerful navy; being further convinced that the naval power of any country is strong or weak in proportion to the extent of its mercantile marine and its sea fisheries, they enacted a law that Hanseatic goods should be conveyed only on board Hanseatic vessels, and established extensive sea fisheries. The English navigation laws were copied from those of the Hanseatic League, just as the latter were an imitation of those of Venice.(1*)

England in that respect only followed the example of those who were her forerunners in acquiring supremacy at sea. Yet the proposal to enact a navigation Act in the time of the Long Parliament was then treated as a novel one. Adam Smith appears in his comment on this Act(2*) not to have known, or to have refrained from stating, that already for centuries before that time and on various occasions the attempt had been made to introduce similar restrictions. A proposal to that effect made by Parliament in 1461 was rejected by Henry VI, and a similar one made by James I, rejected by Parliament;(3*) indeed, long before these two proposals (viz. in 1381) such restrictions had been actually imposed by Richard II, though they soon proved inoperative and passed into oblivion. The nation was evidently not then ripe for such legislation. Navigation laws, like other measures for protecting native industry, are so rooted in the very nature of those nations who feel themselves fitted for future industrial and commercial greatness, that the United States of North America before they had fully won their independence had already at the instance of James Madison introduced restrictions on foreign shipping, and undoubtedly with not less great results (as will be seen in a future chapter) than England had derived from them a hundred and fifty years before.

The northern princes, impressed with the benefits which trade with the Hansards promised to yield to them — inasmuch as it gave them the means not only of disposing of the surplus products of their own territories, and of obtaining in exchange much better manufactured articles than were produced at home, but also of enriching their treasuries by means of import and export duties,(4*) and of diverting to habits of industry their subjects who were addicted to idleness, turbulence, and riot — considered it as a piece of good fortune whenever the Hansards established factories on their territory, and endeavoured to induce them to do so by wanting them privileges and favours of every kind. The kings of England were conspicuous above all other sovereigns in this respect.

The trade of England (says Hume) was formerly entirely in the hands of foreigners, but especially of the 'Easterlings'(5*) whom Henry III constituted a corporation, to whom he granted privileges, and whom he freed from restrictions and import duties to which other foreign merchants were liable. The English at that time were so inexperienced in commerce that from the time of Edward II the Hansards, under the title of 'Merchants of the Steelyard', monopolised the entire foreign trade of the kingdom. And as they conducted it exclusively in their own ships, the shipping interest of England was in a very pitiable condition.(6*)

Some German merchants, viz. those of Cologne, after they had for a long time maintained commercial intercourse with England, at length established in London, in the year 1250, at the invitation of the King, the factory which became so celebrated under the name of 'The Steelyard' an institution which at first was so influential in promoting culture and industry in England, but afterwards excited so much national jealousy, and which for 375 years, until its ultimate dissolution, was the cause of such warm and long-continued conflicts.

England formerly stood in similar relations with the Hanseatic League to those in which Poland afterwards stood with the Dutch, and Germany with the English; she supplied them with wool, tin, hides, butter, and other mineral and agricultural products, and received manufactured articles in exchange. The Hansards conveyed the raw products which they obtained from England and the northern states to their establishment at Bruges (founded in 1252), and exchanged them there for Belgian cloths and other manufactures, and for Oriental products and manufactures which came from Italy, which latter they carried back to all the countries bordering on the northern seas.

A third factory of theirs, at Novgorod in Russia (established in 1272), supplied them with furs, flax, hemp, and other raw products in exchange for manufactures. A fourth factory, at Bergen in Norway (also founded in 1272), was occupied principally with fisheries and trade in train oil and fish products.(7*)

The experience of all nations in all times teaches us that nations, so long as they remain in a state of barbarism, derive enormous benefit from free and unrestricted trade, by which they can dispose of the products of the chase and those of their pastures, forests, and agriculture — in short, raw products of every kind; obtaining in exchange better clothing materials, machines, and utensils, as well as the precious metals — the great medium of exchange and hence that at first they regard free trade with approval. But experience also shows that those very nations, the farther advances that they make for themselves in culture and in industry, regard such a system of trade with a less favourable eye, and that at last they come to regard it as injurious and as a hindrance to their further progress. Such was the case with the trade between England and the Hansards. A century had scarcely elapsed from the foundation of the factory of the 'Steelyard' when Edward III conceived the opinion that a nation might do something more useful and beneficial than to export raw wool and import woollen cloth. He therefore endeavoured to attract Flemish weavers into England by granting them all kinds of privileges; and as soon as a considerable number of them had got to work, he issued a prohibition against wearing any articles made of foreign cloth.(8*)

The wise measures of this king were seconded in the most marvellous manner by the foolish policy pursued by the rulers of other countries — a coincidence which has not unfrequently to be noted in commercial history. If the earlier rulers of Flanders and Brabant did everything in their power to raise their native industry to a flourishing condition, the later ones did everything that was calculated to make the commercial and manufacturing classes discontented and to incite them to emigration.(9*)

In the year 1413 the English woollen industry had already made such progress that Hume could write respecting that period, 'Great jealousy prevailed at this time against foreign merchants, and a number of restrictions were imposed on their trade, as, for instance, that they were required to lay out in the purchase of goods produced in England the whole value which they realized from articles which they imported into it.(10*)

Under Edward IV this jealousy of foreign traders rose to such a pitch that the importation of foreign cloth, and of many other articles, was absolutely prohibited.(11*)

Notwithstanding that the king was afterwards compelled by the Hansards to remove this prohibition, and to reinstate them in their ancient privileges, the English woollen manufacture appears to have been greatly promoted by it, as is noted by Hume in treating of the reign of Henry VII, who came to the throne half a century later than Edward IV.

'The progress made in industry and the arts imposed limits, in a much more effective way than the rigour of laws could do, to the pernicious habit of the nobility of maintaining a great number of servants. Instead of vying with one another in the number and valour of their retainers, the nobility were animated by another kind of rivalry more in accordance with the spirit of civilisation, inasmuch as they now sought to excel one another in the beauty of their houses, the elegance of their equipages, and the costliness of their furniture. As the people could no longer loiter about in pernicious idleness, in the service of their chieftains and patrons, they became compelled, by learning some kind of handiwork, to make themselves useful to the community. Laws were again enacted to prevent the export of the precious metals, both coined and uncoined; but as these were well known to be inoperative, the obligation was again imposed on foreign merchants to lay out the whole proceeds of goods imported by them, in articles of English manufacture.'(12*)

In the time of Henry VIII the prices of all articles of food had considerably risen, owing to the great number of foreign manufacturers in London; a sure sign of the great benefit which the home agricultural industry derived from the development of home manufacturing industry.

The king, however, totally misjudging the causes and the operation of this phenomenon, gave ear to the unjust complaints of the English against the foreign manufacturers, whom the former perceived to have always excelled themselves in skill, industry, and frugality. An order of the Privy Council decreed the expulsion of 15,000 Belgian artificers, 'because they had made all provisions dearer, and had exposed the nation to the risk of a famine.' In order to strike at the root of this evil, laws were enacted to limit personal expenditure, to regulate the style of dress, the prices of provisions, and the rate of wages. This policy naturally was warmly approved by the Hansards, who acted towards this king in the same spirit of good-will which they had previously Displayed towards all those former kings of England whose policy had favoured their interests, and which in our days the English display towards the kings of Portugal — they placed their ships of war at his disposition. During this king's whole reign the trade of the Hansards with England was very active. They possessed both ships and capital, and knew, not less cleverly than the English do in our days, how to acquire influence over peoples and governments who did not thoroughly understand their own interests. Only their arguments rested on quite a different basis from those of the trade monopolists of our day. The Hansards based their claim to supply all countries with manufactures on actual treaties and on immemorial possession of the trade, whilst the English in our day base a similar claim on a mere theory, which has for its author one of their own Custom-house officials. The latter demand in the name of a pretended science, what the former claimed in the name of actual treaties and of justice.

In the reign of Edward VI the Privy Council sought for and found pretexts for abolishing the privileges of the 'Merchants of the Steelyard.' The Hansards made strong protests against this innovation. But the Privy Council persevered in its determination, and the step was soon followed by the most beneficial results to the nation. The English merchants possessed great advantages over the foreign ones, on account of their position as dwellers in the country, in the purchase of cloths, wool, and other articles, advantages which up to that time they had not so clearly perceived as to induce them to venture into competition with such a wealthy company. But from the time when all foreign merchants were subjected to the same commercial restrictions, the English were stimulated to enterprise, and the spirit of enterprise was diffused over the whole kingdom.(13*)

After the Hansards had continued for some years to be entirely excluded from a market which they had for three centuries previously possessed as exclusively as England in our days possesses the markets of Germany and the United States, they were reinstated by Queen Mary in all their ancient privileges owing to representations made by the German Emperor.(14*) But their joy was this time of short duration. Being earnestly Desirous not merely of maintaining these privileges, but of increasing them, they made strong complaints at the beginning of the reign of Elizabeth of the treatment to which they had been subjected under Edward VI and Mary. Elizabeth prudently replied that 'she had no power to alter anything, but she would willingly protect them still in the possession of those privileges and immunities which they then possessed.' This reply, however, did not satisfy them at all. Some time after-wards their trade was further suspended, to the great advantage of the English merchants, who now had an opportunity of showing of what they were capable; they gained control over the entire export trade of their own country, and their efforts were crowned with complete success. They divided themselves into 'staplers and merchant adventurers,' the former carrying on business in some one place, the latter seeking their fortune in foreign cities and states with cloth and other English manu-factures. This excited the jealousy of the Hansards so greatly, that they left no means untried to draw down on the English traders the ill opinion of other nations. At length, on August 1, 1597, they gained an imperial edict, by which all trade within the German Empire was forbidden to English merchants The Queen replied (on January 13, 1598) by proclamation, in consequence of which she sought reprisals by seizing sixty Hanseatic vessels which were engaged in contraband trade with Spain. In taking this step she had at first only intended, by restoring the vessels, to bring about a better understanding with the Hansards. But when she was informed that a general Hanseatic assembly was being held in the city of Lübeck in order to concert measures for harassing the export trade of England, she caused all these vessels with their cargoes to be confiscated, and then released two of them, which she sent to Lübeck with the message that she felt the greatest contempt for the Hanseatic League and all their proceedings and mea-sures.(15*)

Thus Elizabeth acted towards these merchants, who had lent their ships to her father and to so many English kings to fight their battles; who had been courted by all the potentates of Europe; who had treated the kings of Denmark and Sweden as their vassals for centuries, and invited them into their territories and expelled them as they pleased; who had colonised and civilised all the southeastern coasts of the Baltic, and freed all seas from piracy; who not very long before had, with sword in hand, compelled a king of England to recognise their privileges; to whom on more than one occasion English kings had given their crowns in pledge for loans; and who had once carried their cruelty and insolence towards England so far as to drown a hundred English fishermen because they had ventured to approach their fishing grounds. The Hansards, indeed, still possessed sufficient power to have avenged this conduct of the queen of England; but their ancient courage, their mighty spirit of enterprise, the power inspired by freedom and by co-operation, had passed from them. They dwindled gradually into powerlessness until at length, in 1630, their League was formally dissolved, after they had supplicated every court in Europe for import privileges, and had everywhere been repulsed with scorn.

Many external causes, besides the internal ones which we have to mention hereafter, contributed to their fall. Denmark and Sweden sought to avenge themselves for the position of dependence in which they had been so long held by the League, and placed all possible obstructions in the way of its commerce. The czars of Russia had conferred privileges on an English company. The order of Teutonic knights, who had for centuries been the allies as well as (originally) the children of the League, declined and was dissolved. The Dutch and the English drove them out of all markets, and supplanted them in every court. Finally, the discovery of the route to the East indies by the Cape of Good Hope, operated most seriously to their disadvantage.

These leaguers, who during the period of their might and prosperity had scarcely deemed an alliance with the German

Empire as worthy of consideration, now in their time of need betook themselves to the German Reichstag and represented to that body that the English exported annually 200,000 pieces of cloth, of which a great proportion went to Germany, and that the only means whereby the League could regain its ancient privileges in England, was to prohibit the import of English cloth into Germany. According to Anderson, a decree of the Reichstag to that effect was seriously contemplated, if not actually drawn up, but that author asserts that Gilpin, the English ambassador to the Reichstag, contrived to prevent its being passed. A hundred and fifty years after the formal dissolution of the Hanseatic League, so completely had all memory of its former greatness disappeared in the Hanseatic cities that Justus Möser asserts (in some passage in his works) that when he visited those cities, and narrated to their merchants the power and greatness which their predecessors had enjoyed, they would scarcely believe him. Hamburg, formerly the terror of pirates in every sea, and renowned throughout Christendom for the services which she had rendered to civilisation in suppressing sea-robbers, had sunk so low that she had to purchase safety for her vessels by paying an annual tribute to the pirates of Algiers. Afterwards, when the dominion of the seas had passed into the hands of the Dutch another policy became prevalent in reference to piracy. When the Hanseatic League were supreme at sea, the pirate was considered as the enemy of the civilised world, and extirpated wherever that was possible. The Dutch, on the contrary, regarded the corsairs of Barbary as useful partisans, by whose means the marine commerce of other nations could be destroyed in times of peace, to the advantage of the Dutch. Anderson avails himself of the quotation of an observation of De Witt in favour of this policy to make the laconic comment, 'Fas est et ab hoste doceri', a piece of advice which, in spite of its brevity, his countrymen comprehended and followed so well that the English, to the disgrace of Christianity, tolerated even until our days the abominable doings of the sea-robbers on the North African coasts, until the French performed the great service to civilisation of extirpating them.(16*)

The commerce of these Hanseatic cities was not a national one; it was neither based on the equal preponderance and perfect development of internal powers of production, nor sustained by adequate political power. The bonds which held together the members of the League were too lax, the striving among them for predominant power and for separate interests (or, as the Swiss or the Americans would say, the cantonal spirit, the spirit of separate state right) was too predominant, and superseded Hanseatic patriotism, which alone could have caused the general common weal of the League to be considered before the private interests of individual cities. Hence arose jealousies, and not unfrequently treachery. Thus Cologne turned to her own private advantage the hostility of England towards the League, and Hamburg sought to utilise for her own advantage a quarrel which arose between Denmark and Lübeck.

The Hanseatic cities did not base their commerce on the production and consumption, the agriculture or the manufactures, of the land to which their merchants belonged. They had neglected to favour in any way the agricultural industry of their own fatherland, while that of foreign lands was greatly stimulated by their commerce. They found it more convenient to purchase manufactured goods in Belgium, than to establish manufactories in their own country. They encouraged and promoted the agriculture of Poland, the sheep-farming of England, the iron industry of Sweden, and the manufactures of

29

Belgium. They acted for centuries on the maxim which the theoretical economists of our day commend to all nations for adoption — they 'bought only in the cheapest market.' But when the nations from whom they bought, and those to whom they sold, excluded them from their markets, neither their own native agriculture nor their own manufacturing industry was sufficiently developed to furnish employment for their surplus commercial capital. it consequently flowed over into Holland and England, and thus went to increase the industry, the wealth, and the power of their enemies; a striking proof that mere private industry when left to follow its own course does not always promote the prosperity and the power of nations. In their exclusive efforts to gain material wealth, these cities had utterly neglected the promotion of their political interests. During the period of their power, they appeared no longer to belong at all to the German Empire. It flattered these selfish, proud citizens, within their circumscribed territories, to find themselves courted by emperors, kings, and princes, and to act the part of sovereigns of the seas. How easy would it have been for them during the period of their maritime supremacy, in combination with the cities of North Germany, to have founded a powerful Lower House as a counterpoise to the aristocracy of the empire, and by means of the imperial power to have thus brought about national unity — to have united under one nationality the whole sea-coast from Dunkirk to Riga —and by these means to have won and maintained for the German nation supremacy in manufactures, commerce, and maritime power. But in fact, when the sceptre of the seas fell from their grasp, they had not sufficient influence left to induce the German Reichstag to regard their commerce as a matter of national concern. On the contrary, the German aristocracy did all in their power thoroughly to oppress these humbled citizens. Their inland cities fell gradually under the absolute dominion of the various princes, and hence their maritime ones were deprived of their inland connections.

All these faults had been avoided by England. Her merchant shipping and her foreign commerce rested on the solid basis of her native agriculture and native industry; her internal trade developed itself in just proportion to her foreign trade, and individual freedom grew up without prejudice to national unity or to national power: in her case the interests of the Crown, the aristocracy, and the people became consolidated and united in the happiest manner.

If these historical facts are duly considered, can anyone possibly maintain that the English could ever have so widely extended their manufacturing power, acquired such an immeasurably great commerce, or attained such overwhelming naval power, save by means of the commercial policy which they adopted and pursued? No; the assertion that the English have attained to their present commercial eminence and power, not by means of their commercial policy, but in spite of it, appears to us to be one of the greatest falsehoods promulgated in the present century.

Had the English left everything to itself — 'Laissé faire et laissé aller,' as the popular economical school recommends — the merchants of the Steelyard would be still carrying on their trade in London, the Belgians would be still manufacturing cloth for the English, England would have still continued to be the sheep-farm of the Hansards, just as Portugal became the vineyard of England, and has remained so till our days, owing to the stratagem of a cunning diplomatist. Indeed, it is more than probable that without her commercial policy England would never have attained to such a large measure of municipal and individual freedom as she now possesses, for such freedom is the daughter of industry and of wealth.

In view of such historical considerations, how has it happened that Adam Smith has never attempted to follow the history of the industrial and commercial rivalry between the Hanseatic League and England from its origin until its close? Yet some passages in his work show clearly that he was not unacquainted with the causes of the fall of the League and its results. 'A merchant,' he says, 'is not necessarily the citizen of any particular country. It is in a great measure indifferent to him from what place he carries on his trade; and a very trifling disgust will make him remove his capital, and together with it all the industry which it supports, from one country to another. No part of it can be said to belong to any particular country till it has been spread, as it were, over the face of that country, either in buildings or in the lasting improvement of lands. No vestige now remains of the great wealth said to have been possessed by the greater part of the Hanse Towns except in the obscure histories of the thirteenth and fourteenth centuries. it is even uncertain where some of them were situated, or to what towns in Europe the Latin names given to some of them belong.'(17*)

How strange that Adam Smith, having such a clear insight into the secondary causes of the downfall of the Hanseatic League, did not feel himself compelled to examine into its primary causes! For this purpose it would not have been at all necessary to have ascertained the sites where the fallen cities had stood, or to which cities belonged the Latin names in the obscure chronicles. He need not even have consulted those chronicles at all. His own countrymen, Anderson, Macpherson, King, and Hume could have afforded him the necessary explanation.

How, therefore, and for what reason could such a profound

inquirer permit himself to abstain from an investigation at once so interesting and so fruitful in results? We can see no other reason than this — that it would have led to conclusions which would have tended but little to support his principle of absolute free trade. He would infallibly have been confronted with the fact that after free commercial intercourse with the Hansards had raised English agriculture from a state of barbarism, the protective commercial policy adopted by the English nation at the expense of the Hansards, the Belgians, and the Dutch helped England to attain to manufacturing supremacy, and that from the latter, aided by her Navigation Acts, arose her commercial supremacy.

These facts, it would appear, Adam Smith was not willing to know or to acknowledge; for indeed they belong to the category of those inconvenient facts of which J.B. Say observes that they would have proved very adverse to his system.

NOTES:

1. Anderson, Origins of Commerce, pt. I, p. 46.

2. Wealth of Nations, Book IV, ch. ii.

3. Hume, History of England, Part IV, ch. xxi.

4. The revenues of the kings of England were derived at that time more from export duties than from import duties. Freedom of export and duties on imports (viz. of manufactures) betoken at once an advanced state of industry and an enlightened State administration. The governments and countries of the North stood at about the same stage of culture and statemanship as the Sublime Porte does in our day. The Sultan has, notably,

only recently concluded commercial treaties, by which he engages not to tax exports of raw materials and manufactures higher than fourteen per cent but imports not higher than five per cent. And there accordingly that system of finance which professes to regard revenue as its chief object continues in full operation. Those statesmen and public writers who follow or advocate that system ought to betake themselves to Turkey; there they might really stand at the head of the times.

5. The Hansards were formerly termed 'Easterlings' or Eastern merchants, in England, in contradistinction to those of the West, or the Belgians and Dutch. From this term is derived 'sterling' or 'pound sterling', an abbreviation of the word 'Easterlings' because formerly all the coin in circulation in England was that of the Hanseatic League.

6. Hume, History of England, ch. xxxv.

7. M. I. Sartorius, Geschichte der Hansa.

8. II Edward III, cap. 5.

9. Rymer's Foedera, p. 496. De Witte, Interest of Holland, p. 45.

10. Hume, History of England, chap. xxv.

11. Edward IV, cap. iv. The preamble to this Act is so characteristic that we cannot refrain from quoting it verbatim.
    'Whereas to the said Parliament, by the artificers men and women inhabitant and resident in the city of London and in other cities, towns, boroughs and villages within this realm and

Wales, it has been piteously shewed and complained, how that all they in general and every of them he greatly impoverished and much injured and prejudiced of their worldly increase and living, by the great multitude of divers chaffers and wares pertaining to their mysteries and occupations, being fully wrought and ready made to sale, as well by the hand of strangers being the king's enemies as others, brought into this realm and Wales from beyond the sea, as well by merchant strangers as denizens or other persons, whereof the greatest part is deceitful and nothing worth in regard of any man's occupation or profits, by occasion whereof the said artificers cannot live by their mysteries and occupations, as they used to do in times past, but divers of them — as well householders as hirelings and other servants and apprentices — in great number be at this day unoccupied, and do hardly live, in great idleness, poverty and ruin, whereby many inconveniences have grown before this time, and hereafter more are like to come (which God defend), if due remedy be not in their behalf provided.'

12. Hume, chap. xxvi.

13. Hume, chap. xxxv; also Sir J. Hayward, Life and Reign of Edward VI.

14. Hume, chap. xxxvii; Heylyn.

15. Campbell's Lives of the Admirals, vol. i, p. 386.

16. Our author would appear to have forgotten, or else unfairly ignored, the exploits of the British fleet under Lord Exmouth.

17. Smith, Wealth of Nations, Book III, ch. iv.

Chapter 3

The Netherlanders

In respect to temperament and manners, to the origin and language of their inhabitants, no less than to their political connection and geographical position, Holland, Flanders, and Brabant constituted portions of the German Empire. The more frequent visits of Charlemagne and his residence in the vicinity of these countries must have exercised a much more powerful influence on their civilisation than on that of more distant German territories. Furthermore, Flanders and Brabant were specially favoured by nature as respects agriculture and manufactures, as Holland was as respects cattle-farming and commerce.

Nowhere in Germany was internal trade so powerfully aided by extensive and excellent sea and river navigation as in these maritime states. The beneficial effects of these means of water transport on the improvement of agriculture and on the growth of the towns must in these countries, even at an early period, have led to the removal of impediments which hindered their progress and to the construction of artificial canals. The prosperity of Flanders was especially promoted by the circumstance that her ruling Counts recognised the value of public security, of good roads, manufactures, and flourishing cities before all other German potentates, Favoured by the nature of their territory, they devoted themselves with zeal to the extirpation of the robber knights and of wild beasts. Active commercial intercourse between the cities and the country, the extension of cattle-farming, especially of sheep, and of the culture of flax and hemp, naturally followed; and wherever the raw material is abundantly produced, and security of property and of intercourse is maintained, labour and skill for working up that material will soon be found. Meanwhile the Counts of Flanders did not wait until chance should furnish them with woollen weavers, for history informs us that they imported such artificers from foreign countries.

Supported by the reciprocal trade of the Hanseatic League and of Rolland, Flanders soon rose by her woollen manufactures to be the central point of the commerce of the North, just as Venice by her industry and her shipping had become the centre of the commerce of the South. The merchant shipping, and reciprocal trade of the Hanseatic League and the Dutch, together with the manufacturing trade of Flanders, constituted one great whole, a real national industry. A policy of commercial restriction could not in their case be deemed necessary, because as yet no competition had arisen against the manufacturing supremacy of Flanders. That under such circumstances manufacturing industry thrives best under free trade, the Counts of Flanders understood without having read Adam Smith. Quite in the spirit of the present popular theory, Count Robert III, when the King of England requested him to exclude the Scotch from the Flemish markets, replied, 'Flanders has always considered herself a free market for all nations, and it does not consist with her interests to depart from that principle.'

After Flanders had continued for centuries to be the chief manufacturing country, and Bruges the chief market, of Northern Europe, their manufactures and commerce passed over to the neighbouring province of Brabant, because the Counts of Flanders would not continue to grant them those concessions to which in the period of their great prosperity they had laid claim. Antwerp then became the principal seat of commerce, and Louvain the chief manufacturing city of Northern Europe. In consequence of this change of circumstances, the agriculture of Brabant soon rose to a high state of prosperity. The change in early times from payment of imposts in kind to their payment in money, and, above all, the limitation of the feudal system, also tended especially to its advantage.

In the meantime the Dutch, who appeared more and more upon the scene, with united power, as rivals to the Hanseatic League, laid the foundation of their future power at sea. Nature had conferred benefits on this small nation both by her frowns and smiles. Their perpetual contests with the inroads of the sea necessarily developed in them a spirit of enterprise, industry, and thrift, while the land which they had reclaimed and protected by such indescribable exertions must have seemed to them a property to which too much care could not be devoted. Restricted by Nature herself to the pursuits of navigation, of fisheries, and the production of meat, cheese, and butter, the Dutch were compelled to supply their requirements of grain, timber, fuel, and clothing materials by their marine carrying trade, their exports of dairy produce, and their fisheries.

Those were the principal causes why the Hansards were at a later period gradually excluded by the Dutch from the trade with the north-eastern countries. The Dutch required to import far greater quantities of agricultural produce and of timber than did the Hansards, who were chiefly supplied with these articles by the territories immediately adjoining their cities. And, further, the vicinity to Holland of the Belgian manufacturing districts, and of the Rhine with its extensive, fertile, and vine-clad banks, and its stream navigable up to the mountains of Switzerland, constituted great advantages for the Dutch.

It may be considered as an axiom that the commerce and

prosperity of countries on the sea coast is dependent on the greater or less magnitude of the river territories with which they have communication by water.(1*) If we look at the map of Italy, we shall find in the great extent and fertility of the valley of the Po the natural reason why the commerce of Venice so greatly surpassed that of Genoa or of Pisa. The trade of Holland has its chief sources in the territories watered by the Rhine and its tributary streams, and in the same proportion as these territories were much richer and more fertile than those watered by the Elbe and the Weser must the commerce of Holland exceed that of the Hanse Towns. To the advantages above named was added another fortunate incident — the invention by Peter Böckels of the best mode of salting herrings. The best mode of catching and of 'böckelling' these fish (the latter term derived from the inventor) remained for a long period a secret known only to the Dutch, by which they knew how to prepare their herrings with a peculiar excellence surpassing those of all other persons engaged in sea fishery, and secured for themselves a preference in the markets as well as better prices.(2*) Anderson alleges that after the lapse of centuries from the date of these inventions in Holland, the English and Scotch fishermen, notwithstanding their enjoyment of a considerable bounty on export, could not find purchasers for their herrings in foreign markets, eves at much lower prices, in competition with the Dutch. If we bear in mind how great was the consumption of sea fish in all countries before the Reformation, we can well give credit to the fact that at a time when the Hanseatic shipping trade had already begun to decline, the Dutch found occasion for building 2,000 new vessels annually.

From the period when all the Belgian and Batavian provinces were united under the dominion of the House of Burgundy, these countries partly acquired the great benefit of national unity, a circumstance which must not be left out of sight in connection with Holland's success in maritime trade in competition with the cities of Northern Germany. Under the Emperor Charles V the United Netherlands constituted a mass of power and capacity which would have insured to their imperial ruler supremacy over the world, both by land and at sea, far more effectually than all the gold mines on earth and all the papal favours and bulls could have done, had he only comprehended the nature of those powers and known how to direct and to make use of them.

Had Charles V cast away from him the crown of Spain as a man casts away a burdensome stone which threatens to drag him down a precipice, how different would have been the destiny of the Dutch and the German peoples! As Ruler of the United Netherlands, as Emperor of Germany, and as Head of the Reformation, Charles possessed all the requisite means, both material and intellectual, for establishing the mightiest industrial and commercial empire, the greatest military and naval power which had ever existed — a maritime power which would have united under one flag all the shipping from Dunkirk as far as Riga.

The conception of but one idea, the exercise of but one man's will, were all that were seeded to have raised Germany to the position of the wealthiest and mightiest empire in the world, to have extended her manufacturing and commercial supremacy over every quarter of the globe, and probably to have maintained it thus for many centuries.

Charles V and his morose son followed the exactly opposite policy. Placing themselves at the head of the fanatical party, they made it their chief object to hispanicise the Netherlands. The result of that policy is matter of history. The northern

Dutch provinces, strong by means of the element over which they were supreme, conquered their independence. In the southern provinces industry, the arts, and commerce, perished under the hand of the executioner, save only where they managed to escape that fate by emigrating to other countries. Amsterdam became the central point of the world's commerce instead of Antwerp. The cities of Holland, which already at an earlier period, in consequence of the disturbances in Brabant, had attracted a great number of Belgian woollen weavers, had now not room enough to afford refuge to all the Belgian fugitives, of whom a great number were consequently compelled to emigrate to England and to Saxony.

The struggle for liberty begot in Holland an heroic spirit at sea, to which nothing appeared too difficult or too adventurous, while on the contrary the spirit of fanaticism enfeebled the very nerves of Spain. Holland enriched herself principally by privateering against Spain, especially by the capture of the Spanish treasure fleets. By that means she carried on an enormous contraband trade with the Peninsula and with Belgium. After the union of Portugal with Spain, Holland became possessed of the most important Portuguese colonies in the East indies, and acquired a part of Brazil. Up to the first half of the seventeenth century the Dutch surpassed the English in respect of manufactures and of colonial possessions, of commerce and of navigation, as greatly as in our times the English have surpassed the French in these respects. But with the English Revolution a mighty change developed itself. The spirit of freedom had become only a citizen spirit in Holland. As in all mere mercantile aristocracies, all went on well for a time; so long as the preservation of life and limbs and of property, and mere material advantages, were the objects clearly in view, they showed themselves capable of great deeds. But statesmanship of a more profound character was beyond their ken. They did not perceive that the supremacy which they had won, could only be maintained if it were based on a great nationality and supported by a mighty national spirit. On the other hand, those states which had developed their nationality on a large scale by means of monarchy, but which were yet behindhand in respect of commerce and industry, became animated by a sentiment of shame that so small a country as Holland should act the part of master over them in manufactures and commerce, in fisheries, and naval power. In England this sentiment was accompanied by all the energy of the new-born Republic. The Navigation Laws were the challenge glove which the rising supremacy of England cast into the face of the reigning supremacy of Holland. And when the conflict came, it became evident that the English nationality was of far larger calibre than that of the Dutch. The result could not remain doubtful.

The example of England was followed by France. Colbert had estimated that the entire marine transport trade employed about 20,000 vessels, of which 16,000 were owned by the Dutch — a number altogether out of proportion for so small a nation. In consequence of the succession of the Bourbons to the Spanish throne, France was enabled to extend her trade over the Peninsula (to the great disadvantage of the Dutch), and equally so in the Levant. Simultaneously the protection by France of her native manufactures, navigation, and fisheries, made immense inroads on the industry and commerce of Holland.

England had gained from Holland the greater part of the trade of the latter with the northern European states, her contraband trade with Spain and the Spanish colonies, and the greater part of her trade with the East and West Indies, and of her fisheries. But the most serious blow was inflicted on her by the

Methuen Treaty of 1703. From that the commerce of Holland with Portugal, the Portuguese colonies, and the East indies, received a deadly wound.

When Holland thus commenced to lose so large a portion of her foreign trade, the same result took place which had previously been experienced by the Hanseatic cities and by Venice : the material and mental capital which could now find no employment in Holland, was diverted by emigration or in the shape of loans to those countries which had acquired the supremacy from Holland which she had previously possessed.

If Holland in union with Belgium, with the Rhenish districts, and with North Germany, had constituted one national territory, it would have been difficult for England and France to have weakened her naval power, her foreign commerce, and her internal industry by wars and by commercial policy, as they succeeded in doing. A nation such as that would have been, could have placed in competition with the commercial systems of other nations a commercial system of her own. And if owing to the development of the manufactures of those other nations her industry suffered some injury, her own internal resources, aided by founding colonies abroad, would have abundantly made good that loss. Holland suffered decline because she, a mere strip of sea coast, inhabited by a small population of German fishermen, sailors, merchants, and dairy farmers, endeavoured to constitute herself a national power, while she considered and acted towards the inland territory at her back (of which she properly formed a part) as a foreign land.

The example of Holland, like that of Belgium, of the Hanseatic cities, and of the italian republics, teaches us that mere private industry does not suffice to maintain the commerce, industry, and wealth of entire states and nations, if the public circumstances under which it is carried on are unfavourable to it; and further, that the greater part of the productive powers of individuals are derived from the political constitution of the government and from the power of the nation. The agricultural industry of Belgium became flourishing again under Austrian rule. When united to France her manufacturing industry rose again to its ancient immense extent. Holland by herself was never in a position to establish and maintain an independent commercial system of her own in competition with great nations. But when by means of her union with Belgium after the general peace (in 1815) her internal resources, population, and national territory were increased to such an extent that she could rank herself among the great nationalities, and became possessed in herself of a great mass and variety of productive powers, we see the protective system established also in the Netherlands, and under its influence agriculture, manufactures, and commerce make a remarkable advance. This union has now been again dissolved (owing to causes which lie outside the scope and purpose of our present work), and thus the protective system in Holland has been deprived of the basis on which it rested, while in Belgium it is still maintained.

Holland is now maintained by her colonies and by her transport trade with Germany. But the next great naval war may easily deprive her of the former; and the more the German Zollverein attains to a clear perception of its interests, and to the exercise of its powers, the more clearly will it recognize the necessity of including Holland within the Zollverein.

NOTES:

1. The construction of good roads, and still more of railways, which has taken place in quite recent times, has materially

45

modified this axiom.

2. It has been recently stated that the excellence of the Dutch herrings is attributable not only to the superior methods above named, but also to the casks in which they are 'böckelled' and exported being constructed of oak.

Chapter 4

The English

In our account of the Hanseatic League we have shown how in England agriculture and sheep farming have been promoted by foreign trade; how at a subsequent period, through the immigration of foreign artificers, fleeing from persecution in their native land, and also owing to the fostering measures adopted by the British Government, the English woollen manufacturing industry had gradually attained to a flourishing condition; and how, as a direct consequence of that progress in manufacturing industry, as well as of the wise and energetic measures adopted by Queen Elizabeth, all the foreign trade which formerly had been monopolised by foreigners had been successfully diverted into the hands of the merchants at home.

before we continue our exposition of the development of English national economy from the point where we left off in Chapter 2, we venture here to make a few remarks as to the origin of British industry.

The source and origin of England's industrial and commercial greatness must be traced mainly to the breeding of sheep and to the woollen manufacture.

before the first appearance of the Hansards on British soil the agriculture of England was unskilful and her sheep farming of little importance. There was a scarcity of winter fodder for the cattle, consequently a large proportion had to be slaughtered in autumn, and hence both stock and manure were alike deficient. Just as in all uncultivated territories — as formerly in

47

Germany, and in the uncleared districts, of America up to the present time —hog breeding furnished the principal supply of meat, and that for obvious reasons. The pigs needed little care — foraged for themselves, and found a plentiful supply of food on the waste lands and in the forests; and by keeping only a moderate number of breeding sows through the winter, one was sure in the following spring of possessing considerable herds.

but with the growth of foreign trade hog breeding diminished, sheep farming assumed larger proportions, and agriculture and the breeding of horned cattle rapidly improved.

Hume, in his 'History of England,'(1*) gives a very interesting account of the condition of English agriculture at the beginning of the fourteenth century:

'In the year 1327 Lord Spencer counted upon 63 estates in his possession, 28,000 sheep, 1,000 oxen, 1,200 cows, 560 horses, and 2,000 hogs: giving a proportion of 450 sheep, 35 head of cattle, 9 horses, and 22 hogs to each estate.'

From this statement we may perceive how greatly, even in those early days, the number of sheep in England exceeded that of all the other domestic animals put together. The great advantages derived by the English aristocracy from the business of sheep farming gave them an interest in industry and in improved methods of agriculture even at that early period, when noblemen in most Continental states knew no better mode of utilising the greater part of their possessions than by preserving large herds of deer, and when they knew no more honourable occupation than harassing the neighbouring cities and their trade by hostilities of various kinds.

And at this period, as has been the case in Hungary more recently, the flocks so greatly increased that many estates could boast of the possession of from 10,000 to 24,000 sheep. Under these circumstances it necessarily followed that, under the protection afforded by the measures introduced by Queen Elizabeth, the woollen manufacture, which had already progressed very considerably in the days of former English rulers, should rapidly reach a very high degree of prosperity.(2*)

In the petition of the Hansards to the Imperial Diet, mentioned in Chapter II, which prayed for the enactment of retaliatory measures, England's export of cloth was estimated at 200,000 pieces; while in the days of James I the total value of English cloths exported had already reached the prodigious amount of two million pounds sterling, while in the year 1354 the total money value of the wool exported had amounted only to 277,000 l., and that of all other articles of export to no more than 16,400 l. Down to the reign of the last-named monarch the great bulk of the cloth manufactured in England used to be exported to belgium in the rough state and was there dyed and dressed; but owing to the measures of protection and encouragement introduced under James I and Charles I the art of dressing cloth in England attained so high a pitch of perfection that thenceforward the importation of the finer descriptions of cloth nearly ceased, while only dyed and finely dressed cloths were exported.

In order fully to appreciate the importance of these results of the English commercial policy, it must be here observed that, prior to the great development of the linen, cotton, silk, and iron manufactures in recent times, the manufacture of cloth constituted by far the largest proportion of the medium of exchange in the trade with all European nations, particularly with the northern kingdoms, as well as in the commercial intercourse with the Levant and the East and West Indies. To what a great extent this was the case we may infer from the undoubted fact that as far back as the days of James I the export of woollen manufactures represented nine-tenths of all the English exports put together.(3*)

This branch of manufacture enabled England to drive the Hanseatic League out of the markets of Russia, Sweden, Norway, and Denmark, and to acquire for herself the best part of the profits attaching to the trade with the Levant and the East and West Indies. It was this industry that stimulated that of coal mining, which again gave rise to an extensive coasting trade and the fisheries, both which, as constituting the basis of naval power, rendered possible the passing of the famous Navigation Laws which really laid the foundation of England's maritime supremacy. It was round the woollen industry of England that all other branches of manufacture grew up as round a common parent stem; and it thus constitutes the foundation of England's greatness in industry, commerce, and naval power.

At the same time the other branches of English manufacture were in no way neglected. Already under the reign of Elizabeth the importation of metal and leather goods, and of a great many other manufactured articles, had been prohibited, while the immigration of German miners and metal workers was encouraged. Formerly ships had been bought of the Hansards or were ordered to be built in the baltic ports. But she contrived, by restrictions on the one hand and encouragements on the other, to promote shipbuilding at home.

The timber required for the purpose was brought to England from the baltic ports, whereby again a great impetus was given to the British export trade to those regions.

The herring fishery had been learned from the Dutch, whale fishing from the dwellers on the shores of the Bay of Biscay; and both these fisheries were now stimulated by means of bounties. James I more particularly took a lively interest in the encouragement of shipbuilding and of fisheries. Though we may smile at his unceasing exhortations to his people to eat fish, yet we must do him the justice to say that he very clearly perceived on what the future greatness of England depended. The immigration into England, moreover, of the Protestant artificers who had been driven from Belgium and France by Philip II and Louis XIV gave to England an incalculable increase of industrial skill and manufacturing capital. To these men England owes her manufactures of fine woollen cloth, her progress in the arts of making hats, linen, glass, paper, silk, clocks and watches, as well as a part of her metal manufacture; branches of industry which she knew how speedily to increase by means of prohibition and high duties.

The island kingdom borrowed from every country of the Continent its skill in special branches of industry, and planted them on English soil, under the protection of her customs system. Venice had to yield (amongst other trades in articles of luxury) the art of glass manufacture, while Persia had to give up the art of carpet weaving and dyeing.

Once possessed of any one branch of industry, England bestowed upon it sedulous care and attention, for centuries treating it as a young tree which requires support and care. Whoever is not yet convinced that by means of diligence, skill, and economy, every branch of industry must become profitable in time — that in any nation already advanced in agriculture and civilisation, by means of moderate protection, its infant manufactures, however defective and dear their productions at first may be, can by practice, experience, and internal competition readily attain ability to equal in every respect the older productions of their foreign competitors; whoever is ignorant that the success of one particular branch of industry depends on that of several other branches, or to what a high degree a nation can develop its productive powers, if she takes care that each successive generation shall continue the work of industry where former generations have left it; let him first study the history of English industry before he ventures to frame theoretical systems, or to give counsel to practical statesmen to whose hands is given the power of promoting the weal or the woe of nations.

Under George I English statesmen had long ago clearly perceived the grounds on which the greatness of the nation depends. At the opening of Parliament in 1721, the King is made to say by the Ministry, that 'it is evident that nothing so much contributes to promote the public well-being as the exportation of manufactured goods and the importation of foreign raw material.(4*)

This for centuries had been the ruling maxim of English commercial policy, as formerly it had been that of the commercial policy of the Venetian Republic. It is in force at this day (1841) just as it was in the days of Elizabeth. The fruits it has borne lie revealed to the eyes of the whole world. The theorists have since contended that England has attained to wealth and power not by means of, but in spite of, her commercial policy. As well might they argue that trees have grown to vigour and fruitfulness, not by means of, but in spite of, the props and fences with which they had been supported when they were first planted.

Nor does English history supply less conclusive evidence of the intimate connection subsisting between a nation's general political policy and political economy. Clearly the rise and growth of manufactures in England, with the increase of population resulting from it, tended to create an active demand for salt fish and for coals, which led to a great increase of the mercantile marine devoted to fisheries and the coasting trade. Both the fisheries and the coasting trade were previously in the hands of the Dutch. Stimulated by high customs duties and by

52

bounties, the English now directed their own energies to the fishery trade, and by the Navigation Laws they secured chiefly to British sailors not only the transport of sea-borne coal, but the whole of the carrying trade by sea. The consequent increase in England's mercantile marine led to a proportionate augmentation of her naval power, which enabled the English to bid defiance to the Dutch fleet. Shortly after the passing of the Navigation Laws, a naval war broke out between England and Holland, whereby the trade of the Dutch with countries beyond the English Channel suffered almost total suspension, while their shipping in the North Sea and the Baltic was almost annihilated by English privateers. Hume estimates the number of Dutch vessels which thus fell into the hands of English cruisers at 1,600, while Davenant, in his 'Report on the Public Revenue,' assures us that in the course of the twenty-eight years next following the passing of the English Navigation Laws, the English shipping trade had increased to double its previous extent.(5*)

Amongst the more important results of the Navigation Laws, the following deserve special mention, viz.:

1. The expansion of the English trade with all the northern kingdoms, with Germany and Belgium (export of manufactures and import of raw material), from which, according to Anderson's account, up to the year 1603 the English had been almost entirely shut out by the Dutch.

2. An immense extension of the contraband trade with Spain and Portugal, and their West Indian colonies.

3. A great increase of England's herring and whale fisheries, which the Dutch had previously almost entirely monopolised.

4. The conquest of the most important English colony in the West Indies — Jamaica — in 1655; and with that, the command of the West Indian sugar trade.

5. The conclusion of the Methuen Treaty (1703) with Portugal, of which we have fully treated in the chapters devoted to Spain and Portugal in this work. By the operation of this treaty the Dutch and the Germans were entirely excluded from the important trade with Portugal and her colonies: Portugal sank into complete political dependence upon England, while England acquired the means, through the gold and silver earned in her trade with Portugal, of extending enormously her own commercial intercourse with China and the East Indies, and thereby subsequently of laying the foundation for her great Indian empire, and dispossessing the Dutch from their most important trading stations.

The two results last enumerated stand in intimate connection one with the other. And the skill is especially noteworthy with which England contrived to make these two countries — Portugal and India — the instruments of her own future greatness. Spain and Portugal had in the main little to dispose of besides the precious metals, while the requirements of the East, with the exception of cloths, consisted chiefly of the precious metals. So far everything suited most admirably. But the East had principally only cotton and silk manufactures to offer in exchange, and that did not fit in with the principle of the English Ministry before referred to, namely, to export manufactured articles and import raw materials. How, then, did they act under the circumstances? Did they rest content with the profits accruing from the trade in cloths with Portugal and in cotton and silk manufactures with India? By no means. The English Ministers saw farther than that.

Had they sanctioned the free importation into England of Indian cotton and silk goods, the English cotton and silk manufactories must of necessity soon come to a stand. India had not only the advantage of cheaper labour and raw material, but also the experience, the skill, and the practice of centuries. The effect of these advantages could not fail to tell under a system of free competition.

But England was unwilling to found settlements in Asia in order to become subservient to Asia in manufacturing industry. She strove for commercial supremacy, and felt that of two countries maintaining free trade between one another, that one would be supreme which sold manufactured goods, while that one would be subservient which could only sell agricultural produce. In her North American colonies England had already acted on those principles in disallowing the manufacture in those colonies of even a single horseshoe nail, and, still more, that no horseshoe nails made there should be imported into England. How could it be expected of her that she would give up her own market for manufactures, the basis of her future greatness, to a people so numerous, so thrifty, so experienced and perfect in the old systems of manufacture as the Hindoos?

Accordingly, England prohibited the import of the goods dealt in by her own factories, the Indian cotton and silk fabrics.(6*) The prohibition was complete and peremptory. Not so much as a thread of them would England permit to be used. She would have none of these beautiful and cheap fabrics, but preferred to consume her own inferior and more costly stuffs. She was, however, quite willing to supply the Continental nations with the far finer fabrics of India at lower prices, and willingly yielded to them all the benefit of that cheapness; she herself would have none of it.

Was England a fool in so acting? Most assuredly, according to the theories of Adam Smith and J. B. Say the Theory of Values. For, according to them, England should have bought what she required where she could buy them cheapest and best: it was an act of folly to manufacture for herself goods at a greater cost than she could buy them at elsewhere, and at the same time give away that advantage to the Continent.

The case is quite the contrary, according to our theory, which we term the Theory of the Powers of Production, and which the English Ministry, without having examined the foundation on which it rests, yet practically adopted when enforcing their maxim of importing produce and exporting fabrics.

The English Ministers cared not for the acquisition of low-priced and perishable articles of manufacture, but for that of a more costly but enduring manufacturing power.

They have attained their object in a brilliant degree. At this day England produces seventy million pounds' worth of cotton and silk goods, and supplies all Europe, the entire world, India itself included, with British manufactures. Her home production exceeds by fifty or a hundred times the value of her former trade in Indian manufactured goods.

What would it have profited her had she been buying for a century the cheap goods of Indian manufacture?

And what have they gained who purchased those goods so cheaply of her? The English have gained power, incalculable power, while the others have gained the reverse of power.

That in the face of results like these, historically attested upon unimpeachable evidence, Adam Smith should have expressed so warped a judgment upon the Navigation Laws, can only be accounted for upon the same principle on which we shall in another chapter explain this celebrated author's fallacious conclusions respecting commercial restrictions. These facts stood in the way of his pet notion of unrestricted free trade. It was therefore necessary for him to obviate the objection that could be adduced against his principle from the effects of the Navigation Laws, by drawing a distinction between their political objects and their economical objects. He maintained

that, although the Navigation Laws had been politically necessary and beneficial, yet that they were economically prejudicial
and injurious. How little this distinction can be justified by the
nature of things or by experience, we trust to make apparent in
the course of this treatise.

J. B. Say, though he might have known better from the
experience of North America, here too, as in every instance
where the principles of free trade and protection clash, goes
still farther than his predecessor. Say reckons up what the cost
of a sailor to the French nation is, owing to the fishery bounties, in order to show how wasteful and unremunerative these
bounties are.

The subject of restrictions upon navigation constitutes a
formidable stumbling-block in the path of the advocates of
unrestricted free trade, which they are only too glad to pass
over in silence, especially if they are members of the mercantile
community in seaport towns.

The truth of the matter is this. Restrictions on navigation are
governed by the same law as restrictions upon any other kind of
trade. Freedom of navigation and the carrying trade conducted
by foreigners are serviceable and welcome to communities in
the early stages of their civilisation, so long as their agriculture
and manufactures still remain undeveloped. Owing to want of
capital and of experienced seamen, they are willing to abandon
navigation and foreign trade to other nations. Later on, however, when they have developed their producing power to a
certain point and acquired skill in shipbuilding and navigation,
then they will desire to extend their foreign trade, to carry it on
in their own ships, and become a naval power themselves.
Gradually their own mercantile marine grows to such a degree
that they feel themselves in a position to exclude the foreigner
and to conduct their trade to the most distant places by means

of their own vessels. Then the time has come when, by means of restrictions on navigation, a nation can successfully exclude the more wealthy, more experienced, and more powerful foreigner from participation in the profits of that business. When the highest degree of progress in navigation and maritime power has been reached, a new era will set in, no doubt; and such was that stage of advancement which Dr Priestley had in his mind when he wrote 'that the time may come when it may be as politic to repeal this Act as it was to make it.'(7*)

Then it is that, by means of treaties of navigation based upon equality of rights, a nation can, on the one hand, secure undoubted advantages as against less civilised nations, who will thus be debarred from introducing restrictions on navigation in their own special behalf; while, on the other hand, it will thereby preserve its own seafaring population from sloth, and spur them on to keep pace with other countries in shipbuilding and in the art of navigation. While engaged in her struggle for supremacy, Venice was doubtless greatly indebted to her policy of restrictions on navigation; but as soon as she had acquired supremacy in trade, manufactures, and navigation, it was folly to retain them. For owing to them she was left behind in the race, both as respects shipbuilding, navigation, and seamanship of her sailors, with other maritime and commercial nations which were advancing in her footsteps. Thus England by her policy increased her naval power, and by means of her naval power enlarged the range of her manufacturing and commercial powers, and again, by the latter, there accrued to her fresh accessions of maritime strength and of colonial possessions. Adam Smith, when he maintains that the Navigation Laws have not been beneficial to England in commercial respects, admits that, in any case, these laws have increased her power. And power is more important than wealth. That is indeed the fact. Power is more important than wealth. And why? Simply because national power is a dynamic force by which new productive resources are opened out, and because the forces of production are the tree on which wealth grows, and because the tree which bears the fruit is of greater value than the fruit itself. Power is of more importance than wealth because a nation, by means of power, is enabled not only to open up new productive sources, but to maintain itself in possession of former and of recently acquired wealth, and because the reverse of power — namely, feebleness — leads to the relinquishment of all that we possess, not of acquired wealth alone, but of our powers of production, of our civilisation, of our freedom, nay, even of our national independence, into the hands of those who surpass us in might, as is abundantly attested by the history of the Italian republics, of the Hanseatic League, of the Belgians, the Dutch, the Spaniards, and the Portuguese.

But how came it that, unmindful of this law of alternating action and reaction between political power, the forces of production and wealth, Adam Smith could venture to contend that the Methuen Treaty and the Act of Navigation had not been beneficial to England from a commercial point of view? We have shown how England by the policy which she pursued acquired power, and by her political power gained productive power, and by her productive power gained wealth. Let us now see further how, as a result of this policy, power has been added to power, and productive forces to productive forces.

England has got into her possession the keys of every sea, and
placed a sentry over every nation: over the Germans, Heligoland; over the French, Guernsey and Jersey; over the inhabitants of North America, Nova Scotia and the Bermudas; over Central America, the island of Jamaica; over all countries

bordering on the Mediterranean, Gibraltar, Malta, and the Ionian Islands. She possesses every important strategical position on both the routes to India with the exception of the Isthmus of Suez, which she is striving to acquire; she dominates the Mediterranean by means of Gibraltar, the Red Sea by Aden, and the Persian Gulf by Bushire and Karrack. She needs only the further acquisition of the Dardanelles, the Sound, and the Isthmuses of Suez and Panama, in order to be able to open and close at her pleasure every sea and every maritime highway. Her navy alone surpasses the combined maritime forces of all other countries, if not in number of vessels, at any rate in fighting strength.

Her manufacturing capacity excels in importance that of all other nations. And although her cloth manufactures have increased more than tenfold (to forty-four and a half millions) since the days of James I, we find the yield of another branch of industry, which was established only in the course of the last century, namely, the manufacture of cotton, amounting to a much larger sum, fifty-two and a half millions.(8*)

Not content with that, England is now attempting to raise her linen manufacture, which has been long in a backward state as compared with that of other countries, to a similar position, possibly to a higher one than that of the two above-named branches of industry: it now amounts to fifteen and a half millions sterling. In the fourteenth century, England was still so poor in iron that she thought it necessary to prohibit the exportation of this indispensable metal; she now, in the nineteenth century, manufactures more iron and steel wares than all the other nations on earth (namely, thirty-one millions' worth), while she produces thirty-four millions in value of coal and other minerals. These two sums exceed by over sevenfold the value of the entire gold and silver production of all other nations, which amount to about two hundred and twenty million francs, or nine millions sterling.

At this day she produces more silk goods than all the Italian republics produced in the Middle Ages together, namely, thirteen and a half million pounds. Industries which at the time of Henry VIII and Elizabeth scarcely deserved classification, now yield enormous sums; as, for instance, the glass, china, and stoneware manufactures, representing eleven millions; the copper and brass manufactures, four and a half millions; the manufactures of paper, books, colours, and furniture, fourteen millions.

England produces, moreover, sixteen millions' worth of leather goods, besides ten millions' worth of unenumerated articles. The manufacture of beer and spirituous liquors in England alone greatly exceeds in value the aggregate of national production in the days of James I, namely, forty-seven millions sterling.

The entire manufacturing production of the United Kingdom at the present time, is estimated to amount to two hundred and fifty-nine and a half millions sterling.

As a consequence, and mainly as a consequence, of this gigantic manufacturing production, the productive power of agriculture has been enabled to yield a total value exceeding twice that sum (five hundred and thirty-nine millions sterling).

It is true that for this increase in her power, and in her productive capacity, England is not indebted solely to her commercial restrictions, her Navigation Laws, or her commercial treaties, but in a large measure also to her conquests in science and in the arts.

But how comes it, that in these days one million of English operatives can perform the work of hundreds of millions? It comes from the great demand for manufactured goods which by her wise and energetic policy she has known how to create in foreign lands, and especially in her colonies; from the wise and powerful protection extended to her home industries; from the great rewards which by means of her patent laws she has offered to every new discovery; and from the extraordinary facilities for her inland transport afforded by public roads, canals, and railways.

England has shown the world how powerful is the effect of facilities of transport in increasing the powers of production, and thereby increasing the wealth, the population, and the political power of a nation. She has shown us what a free, industrious, and well-governed community can do in this respect within the brief space of half a century, even in the midst of foreign wars. That which the Italian republics had previously accomplished in these respects was mere child's play. It is estimated that as much as a hundred and eighteen millions sterling have been expended in England upon these mighty instruments of the nation's productive power.

England, however, only commenced and carried out these works when her manufacturing power began to grow strong. Since then, it has become evident to all observers that that nation only whose manufacturing power begins to develop itself upon an extensive scale is able to accomplish such works; that only in a nation which develops concurrently its internal manufacturing and agricultural resources will such costly engines of trade repay their cost; and that in such a nation only will they properly fulfil their purpose.

It must be admitted, too, that the enormous producing capacity and the great wealth of England are not the effect solely of national power and individual love of gain. The people's innate love of liberty and of justice, the energy, the religious and moral character of the people, have a share in it. The constitution of the country, its institutions, the wisdom and power of the Government and of the aristocracy, have a share in it. The geographical position, the fortunes of the country, nay, even good luck, have a share in it.

It is not easy to say whether the material forces exert a greater influence over the moral forces, or whether the moral outweigh the material in their operation; whether the social forces act upon the individual forces the more powerfully, or whether the latter upon the former. This much is certain, however, namely, that between the two there subsists an interchanging sequence of action and reaction, with the result that the increase of one set of forces promotes the increase of the other, and that the enfeeblement of the one ever involves the enfeeblement of the other.

Those who seek for the fundamental causes of England's rise and progress in the blending of Anglo-Saxon with the Norman blood, should first cast a glance at the condition of the country before the reign of Edward III. Where were then the diligence and the habits of thrift of the nation? Those again who would look for them in the constitutional liberties enjoyed by the people will do well to consider how Henry VIII and Elizabeth treated their Parliaments. Wherein did England's constitutional freedom consist under the Tudors? At that period the cities of Germany and Italy enjoyed a much greater amount of individual freedom than the English did.

Only one jewel out of the treasure-house of freedom was preserved by the Anglo-Saxon-Norman race — before other peoples of Germanic origin; and that was the germ from which all the English ideas of freedom and justice have sprung — the right of trial by jury.

While in Italy the Pandects were being unearthed, and the exhumed remains (no doubt of departed greatness and wisdom

63

in their day) were spreading the pestilence of the Codes amongst Continental nations, we find the English Barons declaring they would not hear of any change in the law of the land. What a store of intellectual force did they not thereby secure for the generations to come! How much did this intellectual force subsequently influence the forces of material production!

How greatly did the early banishment of the Latin language from social and literary circles, from the State departments, and the courts of law in England, influence the development of the nation, its legislation, law administration, literature, and industry! What has been the effect upon Germany of the long retention of the Latin in conjunction with foreign Codes, and what has been its effect in Hungary to the present day? What an effect have the invention of gunpowder, the art of printing, the Reformation, the discovery of the new routes to India and of America, had on the growth of English liberties, of English civilisation, and of English industry? Compare with this their effect upon Germany and France. In Germany — discord in the Empire, in the provinces, even within the walls of cities; miserable controversies, barbarism in literature, in the administration of the State and of the law; civil war, persecutions, expatriation, foreign invasion, depopulation, desolation; the ruin of cities, the decay of industry, agriculture, and trade, of freedom and civic institutions; supremacy of the great nobles; decay of the imperial power, and of nationality; severance of the fairest provinces from the Empire. In France — subjugation of the cities and of the nobles in the interest of despotism; alliance with the priesthood against intellectual freedom, but at the same time national unity and power; conquest with its gain and its curse, but, as against that, downfall of freedom and of industry. In England — the rise of cities, progress in agriculture, commerce, and manufactures; subjection of the aristocracy to the law of the land, and hence a preponderating participation by the nobility in the work of legislation, in the administration of the State and of the law, as also in the advantages of industry; development of resources at home, and of political power abroad; internal peace; influence over all less advanced communities; limitation of the powers of the Crown, but gain by the Crown in royal revenues, in splendour and stability. Altogether, a higher degree of well-being, civilisation, and freedom at home, and preponderating might abroad.

But who can say how much of these happy results is attributable to the English national spirit and to the constitution; how much to England's geographical position and circumstances in the past; or again, how much to chance, to destiny, to fortune?

Let Charles V and Henry VIII change places, and, in consequence of a villanous divorce trial, it is conceivable (the reader will understand why we say 'conceivable') that Germany and the Netherlands might have become what England and Spain have become. Place in the position of Elizabeth, a weak woman allying herself to a Philip II, and how would it have fared with the power, the civilisation, and the liberties of Great Britain?

If the force of national character will alone account for everything in this mighty revolution, must not then the greatest share of its beneficial results have accrued to the nation from which it sprang, namely, to Germany? Instead of that, it is just the German nation which reaped nothing save trouble and weakness from this movement in the direction of progress.

In no European kingdom is the institution of an aristocracy more judiciously designed than in England for securing to the nobility, in their relation to the Crown and the commonalty, individual independence, dignity, and stability; to give them a Parliamentary training and position; to direct their energies to patriotic and national aims; to induce them to attract to their own body the élite of the commonalty, to include in their ranks every commoner who earns distinction, whether by mental gifts, exceptional wealth, or great achievements; and, on the other hand, to cast back again amongst the commons the surplus progeny of aristocratic descent, thus leading to the amalgamation of the nobility and the commonalty in future generations. By this process the nobility is ever receiving from the Commons fresh accessions of civic and patriotic energy, of science, learning, intellectual and material resources, while it is ever restoring to the people a portion of the culture and of the spirit of independence peculiarly its own, leaving its own children to trust to their own resources, and supplying the commonalty with incentives to renewed exertion. In the case of the English lord, however large may be the number of his descendants, only one can hold the title at a time. The other members of the family are commoners, who gain a livelihood either in one of the learned professions, or in the Civil Service, in commerce, industry, or agriculture. The story goes that some time ago one of the first dukes in England conceived the idea of inviting all the blood relations of his house to a banquet, but he was fain to abandon the design because their name was legion, notwithstanding that the family pedigree had not reached farther back than for a few centuries. It would require a whole volume to show the effect of this institution upon the spirit of enterprise, the colonisation, the might and the liberties, and especially upon the forces of production of this nation.(9*)

The geographical position of England, too, has exercised an immense influence upon the independent development of the nation. England in its relation to the continent of Europe has ever been a world by itself; and was always exempt from the effects of the rivalries, the prejudices, the selfishness, the passions, and the disasters of her Continental neighbours. To this isolated condition she is mainly indebted for the independent and unalloyed growth of her political constitution, for the undisturbed consummation of the Reformation, and for the secularisation of ecclesiastical property which has proved so beneficial to her industries. To the same cause she is also indebted for that continuous peace, which, with the exception of the period of the civil war, she has enjoyed for a series of centuries, and which enabled her to dispense with standing armies, while facilitating the early introduction of a consistent customs system.

By reason of her insular position, England not only enjoyed immunity from territorial wars, but she also derived immense advantages for her manufacturing supremacy from the Continental wars. Land wars and devastations of territory inflict manifold injury upon the manufactures at the seat of hostilities; directly, by interfering with the farmer's work and destroying the crops, which deprives the tiller of the soil of the means wherewithal to purchase manufactured goods, and to produce raw material and food for the manufacturer; indirectly, by often destroying the manufactories, or at any rate ruining them, because hostilities interfere with the importation of raw material and with the exportation of goods, and because it becomes a difficult matter to procure capital and labour just at the very time when the masters have to bear extraordinary imposts and heavy taxation; and lastly the injurious effects continue to operate even after the cessation of the war, because both capital and individual effort are ever attracted towards agricultural work and diverted from manufactures, precisely in that proportion in which the war may have injured the farmers and their crops, and thereby opened up a more directly profitable field for the employment of capital and of labour than the manufacturing industries would then afford. While in Germany this condition of things recurred twice in every hundred years, and caused German manufactures to retrograde, those of England made uninterrupted progress. English manufacturers, as opposed to their Continental competitors, enjoyed a double and treble advantage whenever England, by fitting out fleets and armies, by subsidies, or by both these means combined, proceeded to take an active part in foreign wars.

We cannot agree with the defenders of unproductive expenditure, namely, of that incurred by wars and the maintenance of large armies, nor with those who insist upon the positively beneficial character of a public debt; but neither do we believe that the dominant school are in the right when they contend that all consumption which is not directly reproductive — for instance, that of war — is absolutely injurious without qualification. The equipment of armies, wars, and the debts contracted for these purposes, may, as the example of England teaches, under certain circumstances, very greatly conduce to the increase of the productive powers of a nation. Strictly speaking, material wealth may have been consumed unproductively, but this consumption may, nevertheless, stimulate manufacturers to extraordinary exertions, and lead to new discoveries and improvements, especially to an increase of productive powers. This productive power then becomes a permanent acquisition; it will increase more and more, while the expense of the war is incurred only once for all.(10*) And thus it may come to pass, under favouring conditions such as have occurred in England, that a nation has gained immeasurably more than it has lost from that very kind of expenditure which theorists hold to be unproductive. That such was really the case with England, may be shown by figures. For in the course of the war, that country had acquired in the cotton manufacture alone a power of production which yields annually a much larger return in value than the amount which the nation has to find to defray the interest upon the increased national debt, not to mention the vast development of all other branches of industry, and the additions to her colonial wealth.

Most conspicuous was the advantage accruing to the English manufacturing interest during the Continental wars, when England maintained army corps on the Continent or paid subsidies. The whole expenditure on these was sent, in the shape of English manufactures, to the seat of war, where these imports then materially contributed to crush the already sorely suffering foreign manufacturers, and permanently to acquire the market of the foreign country for English manufacturing industry. It operated precisely like an export bounty instituted for the benefit of British and for the injury of foreign manufacturers.(11*)

In this way, the industry of the Continental nations has ever suffered more from the English as allies, than from the English as enemies. In support of this statement we need refer only to the Seven Years' War, and to the wars against the French Republic and Empire.

Great, however, as have been the advantages heretofore mentioned, they have been greatly surpassed in their effect by those which England derived from immigrations attracted by her political, religious, and geographical conditions.

As far back as the twelfth century political circumstances induced Flemish woollen weavers to emigrate to Wales. Not many centuries later exiled Italians came over to London to carry on business as money changers and bankers. That from Flanders and Brabant entire bodies of manufacturers thronged to England at various periods, we have shown in Chapter II. From Spain and Portugal came persecuted Jews; from the

Hanse Towns, and from Venice in her decline, merchants who brought with them their ships, their knowledge of business, their capital, and their spirit of enterprise. Still more important were the immigrations of capital and of manufacturers in consequence of the Reformation and the religious persecutions in Spain, Portugal, France, Belgium, Germany, and Italy; as also of merchants and manufacturers from Holland in consequence of the stagnation of trade and industry in that country occasioned by the Act of Navigation and the Methuen Treaty. Every political movement, every war upon the Continent, brought England vast accessions of fresh capital and talents, so long as she possessed the privileges of freedom, the right of asylum, internal tranquillity and peace, the protection of the law, and general well-being. So more recently did the French Revolution and the wars of the Empire; and so did the political commotions, the revolutionary and reactionary movements and the wars in Spain, in Mexico, and in South America. By means of her Patent Laws, England long monopolised the inventive genius of every nation. It is no more than fair that England, now that she has attained the culminating point of her industrial growth and progress, should restore again to the nations of Continental Europe a portion of those productive forces which she originally derived from them.

NOTES:

1. Hume, vol. ii, p. 143.

2. No doubt the decrees prohibiting the export of wool, not to mention the restrictions placed on the trade in wool in markets near the coast, were vexations and unfair; yet at the same time the operated beneficially in the promotion of English industry,

and in the suppression of that of the Flemings.

3. Hume (in 1603). Macpherson, Histoire du Commerce (in 1651).

4. See Ustaritz, Théorie du Commerce, ch. xxviii. Thus we see George I did not want to export goods and import nothing but specie in return, which is stated as the fundamental principle of the so-called 'mercantile system', and which in any case would be absurd. What he desired was to export manufactures and import raw material.

5. Hume, vol. v. p. 39.

6. Anderson for the year 1721.

7. Priestley, Lectures on History and General Policy, Pt. II, p. 289.

8. These and the following figures relating to English statistics are taken from a paper written by McQueen, the celebrated English statistician, and appearing in the July number of Tait's Edinburgh Magazine for the year 1839. Possibly they may be somewhat exaggerated for the moment. But even if so, it is more than probable that the figures as stated will be reached within the present decade.

9. Before his lamented death, the gifted author of this remark, in his Letters on England, read the nobles of his native country a lesson in this respect which they would do well to lay to heart.

10. England's national debt would not be so great an evil as it now appears to us, if England's aristocracy would concede that this burden should be borne by the class who were benefited by the cost of wars, namely, by the rich. McQueen estimates the capitalised value of property in the three kingdoms at 4,000 million pounds sterling, and Martin estimates the capital invested in the colonies at about 2,600 millions sterling. Hence we see that one-ninth part of Englishmen's private property would suffice to cover the entire national debt. Nothing could be more just than such an appropriation, or at least than the payment of the interest on the national debt out of the proceeds of an income tax. The English aristocracy, however, deem it more convenient to provide for this charge by the imposition of taxes upon articles of consumption, by which the existence of the working classes is embittered beyond the point of endurance.

11. See Appendix A.

Chapter 5

The Spaniards and Portuguese

Whilst the English were busied for centuries in raising the structure of their national prosperity upon the most solid foundations, the Spaniards and the Portuguese made a fortune rapidly by means of their discoveries and attained to great wealth in a very short space of time. But it was only the wealth of a spendthrift who had won the first prize in a lottery, whereas the wealth of the English may be likened to the fortune accumulated by the diligent and saving head of a family. The former may for a time appear more to be envied than the latter on account of his lavish expenditure and luxury; but wealth in his case is only a means for prodigality and momentary enjoyment, whereas the latter will regard wealth chiefly as a means of laying a foundation for the moral and material well-being of his latest posterity.

The Spaniards possessed flocks of well-bred sheep at so early a period that Henry I of England was moved to prohibit the importation of Spanish wool in 1172, and that as far back as the tenth and eleventh centuries Italian woollen manufacturers used to import the greater portion of their wool supplies from Spain. Two hundred years before that time the dwellers on the shores of the Bay of Biscay had already distinguished themselves in the manufacture of iron, in navigation, and in fisheries. They were the first to carry on the whale fishery, and even in the year 1619 they still so far excelled the English in that business that they were asked to send fishermen to England to instruct the English in this particular branch of the fishing trade.(1*)

Already in the tenth century, under Abdulrahman III (912 to 950), the Moors had established in the fertile plains around Valencia extensive plantations of cotton, sugar, and rice, and carried on silk cultivation. Cordova, Seville, and Granada contained at the time of the Moors important cotton and silk manufactories.(2*) Valencia, Segovia, Toledo, and several other cities in Castile were celebrated for their woollen manufactures. Seville alone at an early period of history contained as many as 16,000 looms, while the woollen manufactories of Segovia in the year 1552 were employing 13,000 operatives. Other branches of industry, notably the manufacture of arms and of paper, had become developed on a similar scale. In Colbert's day the French were still in the habit of procuring supplies of cloth from Spain.(3*) The Spanish seaport towns were the seat of an extensive trade and of important fisheries, and up to the time of Philip II Spain possessed a most powerful navy. In a word, Spain possessed all the elements of greatness and prosperity, when bigotry, in alliance with despotism, set to work to stifle the high spirit of the nation. The first commencement of this work of darkness was the expulsion of the Jews, and its crowning act the expulsion of the Moors, whereby two millions of the most industrious and well-to-do inhabitants were driven out of Spain with their capital.

While the Inquisition was thus occupied in driving native industry into exile, it at the same time effectually prevented foreign manufacturers from settling down in the country. The discovery of America and of the route round the Cape only increased the wealth of both kingdoms after a specious and ephemeral fashion — indeed, by these events a death-blow was first given to their national industry and to their power. For then, instead of exchanging the produce of the East and West

Indies against home manufactures, as the Dutch and the English subsequently did, the Spaniards and Portuguese purchased manufactured goods from foreign nations with the gold and the silver which they had wrung from their colonies.(4*) They transformed their useful and industrious citizens into slave-dealers and colonial tyrants: thus they promoted the industry; the trade, and the maritime power of the Dutch and English, in whom they raised up rivals who soon grew strong enough to destroy their fleets and rob them of the sources of their wealth. In vain the kings of Spain enacted laws against the exportation of specie and the importation of manufactured goods. The spirit of enterprise, industry, and commerce can only strike root in the soil of religious and political liberty; gold and silver will only abide where industry knows how to attract and employ them.

Portugal, however, under the auspices of an enlightened and powerful minister, did make an attempt to develop her manu-facturing industry, the first results of which strike us with astonishment. That country like Spain, had possessed from time immemorial fine flocks of sheep. Strabo tells us that a fine breed of sheep had been introduced into Portugal from Asia, the cost of which amounted to one talent per head. When the Count of Ereceira became minister in 1681, he conceived the design of establishing cloth manufactories, and of thus working up the native raw material in order to supply the mother coun-try and the colonies with home-manufactured goods. With that view cloth workers were invited from England, and so speedily did the native cloth manufactories flourish in consequence of the protection secured to them, that three years later (in 1684) it became practicable to prohibit the importation of foreign cloths. From that period Portugal supplied herself and her colonies with native goods manufactured of home-grown raw material, and prospered exceedingly in so doing for a period of nineteen years, as attested by the evidence of English writers themselves.(5*)

It is true that even in those days the English gave proof of that ability which at subsequent times they have managed to bring to perfection. In order to evade the tariff restrictions of Portugal, they manufactured woollen fabrics, which slightly differed from cloth though serving the same purpose, and imported these into Portugal under the designation of woollen serges and woollen druggets. This trick of trade was, however, soon detected and rendered innocuous by a decree prohibiting the importation of such goods.(6*) The success of these measures is all the more remarkable because the country, not a very great while before, had been drained of a large amount of capital, which had found its way abroad owing to the expulsion of the Jews, and was suffering especially from all the evils of bigotry, of bad government, and of a feudal aristocracy, which ground down popular liberties and agriculture.(7*)

In the year 1703, after the death of Count Ereceira, however, the famous British ambassador Paul Methuen succeeded in persuading the Portuguese Government that Portugal would be immensely benefited if England were to permit the importation of Portuguese wines at a duty one-third less than the duty levied upon wines of other countries, in consideration of Portugal admitting English cloths at the same rate of import duty (viz. twenty-three per cent.) which had been charged upon such goods prior to the year 1684. It seems as though on the part of the King the hope of an increase in his customs revenue, and on the part of the nobility the hope of an increased income from rents, supplied the chief motives for the conclusion of that commercial treaty in which the Queen of England (Anne) styles the King of Portugal 'her oldest friend and ally' — on much the same principle as the Roman Senate was formerly wont to apply such designations to those rulers who had the misfortune to be brought into closer relations with that assembly.

Directly after the conclusion of this treaty, Portugal was deluged with English manufactures, and the first result of this inundation was the sudden and complete ruin of the Portuguese manufactories — a result which had its perfect counterparts in the subsequent so-called Eden treaty with France and in the abrogation of the Continental system in Germany.

According to Anderson's testimony, the English, even in those days, had become such adepts in the art of understating the value of their goods in their custom-house bills of entry, that in effect they paid no more than half the duty chargeable on them by the tariff.(8*)

'After the repeal of the prohibition,' says 'The British Merchant,' 'we managed to carry away so much of their silver currency that there remained but very little for their necessary occasions; thereupon we attacked their gold.'(9*) This trade the English continued down to very recent times. They exported all the precious metals which the Portuguese had obtained from their colonies, and sent a large portion of them to the East Indies and to China, where, as we saw in Chapter IV, they exchanged them for goods which they disposed of on the continent of Europe against raw materials. The yearly exports of England to Portugal exceed the imports from that country by the amount of one million sterling. This favourable balance of trade lowered the rate of exchange to the extent of fifteen per cent to the disadvantage of Portugal. 'The balance of trade is more favourable to us in our dealings with Portugal than it is with any other country,' says the author of 'The British Merchant' in his dedication to Sir Paul Methuen, the son of the famous minister, 'and our imports of specie from that country have risen to the sum of one and a half millions sterling, whereas formerly they amounted only to 300,000 l.'(10*)

All the merchants and political economists, as well as all the statesmen of England, have ever since eulogised this treaty as the masterpiece of English commercial policy. Anderson himself, who had a clear insight enough into all matters affecting English commercial policy and who in his way always treats of them with great candour call's it 'an extremely fair and advantageous treaty;' nor could he forbear the naïve exclamation, 'May it endure for ever and ever!'(11*)

For Adam Smith alone it was reserved to set up a theory directly opposed to this unanimous verdict, and to maintain that the Methuen Treaty had in no respect proved a special boon to British commerce. Now, if anything will suffice to show the blind reverence with which public opinion has accepted the (partly very paradoxical) views of this celebrated man, surely it is the fact that the particular opinion above mentioned has hitherto been left unrefuted.

In the sixth chapter of his fourth book Adam Smith says, that inasmuch as under the Methuen Treaty the wines of Portugal were admitted upon paying only two-thirds of the duty which was paid on those of other nations, a decided advantage was conceded to the Portuguese; whereas the English, being bound to pay quite as high a duty in Portugal on their exports of cloth as any other nation, had, therefore, no special privilege granted to them by the Portuguese. But had not the Portuguese been previously importing a large proportion of the foreign goods which they required from France, Holland, Germany, and Belgium? Did not the English thenceforth exclusively command the Portuguese market for a manufactured product, the raw material for which they possessed in their own country? Had they not discovered a method of reducing the Portuguese customs duty by one-half? Did not the course of exchange give the English consumer of Portuguese wines a profit of fifteen per cent? Did not the consumption of French and German wines in England almost entirely cease? Did not the Portuguese gold and silver supply the English with the means of bringing vast quantities of goods from India and of deluging the continent of Europe with them? Were not the Portuguese cloth manufactories totally ruined, to the advantage of the English? Did not all the Portuguese colonies, especially the rich one of Brazil, by this means become practically English colonies? Certainly this treaty conferred a privilege upon Portugal, but only in name; whereas it conferred a privilege upon the English in its actual operation and effects. A like tendency underlies all subsequent treaties of commerce negotiated by the English. By profession they were always cosmopolites and philanthropists, while in their aims and endeavours they were always monopolists.

According to Adam Smith's second argument, the English gained no particular advantages from this treaty, because they were to a great extent obliged to send away to other countries the money which they received from the Portuguese for their cloth, and with it to purchase goods there; whereas it would have been far more profitable for them to make a direct exchange of their cloths against such commodities as they might need, and thus by one exchange accomplish that which by means of the trade with Portugal they could only effect by two exchanges. Really, but for the very high opinion which we entertain of the character and the acumen of this celebrated savant, we should in the face of this argument be driven to despair either of his candour or of his clearness of perception. To avoid doing either, nothing is left for us but to bewail the weakness of human nature, to which Adam Smith has paid a rich tribute in the shape of these paradoxical, almost laughable, arguments among other instances; being evidently dazzled by the splendour of the task, so noble in itself, of pleading a justification for absolute freedom of trade.

In the argument just named there is no more sound sense or logic than in the proposition that a baker, because he sells bread to his customers for money, and with that money buys flour from the miller, does an unprofitable trade, because if he had exchanged his bread directly for flour, he would have effected his purpose by a single act of exchange instead of by two such acts. It needs surely no great amount of sagacity to answer such an allegation by hinting that the miller might possibly not want so much bread as the baker could supply him with, that the miller might perhaps understand and undertake baking himself, and that, therefore, the baker's business could not go on at all without these two acts of exchange. Such in effect were the commercial conditions of Portugal and England at the date of the treaty. Portugal received gold and silver from South America in exchange for manufactured goods which she then exported to those regions; but too indolent or too shiftless to manufacture these goods herself, she bought them of the English in exchange for the precious metals. The latter employed the precious metals, in so far as they did not require them for the circulation at home, in exportation to India or China, and bought goods there which they sold again on the European continent, whence they brought home agricultural produce, raw material, or precious metals once again.

We now ask, in the name of common sense, who would have purchased of the English all those cloths which they exported to Portugal, if the Portuguese had chosen either to make them at home or procure them from other countries? The English could not in that case have sold them to Portugal, and to other nations they were already selling as much as those nations would take. Consequently the English would have manufactured so much less cloth than they had been disposing of to the Portuguese; they would have exported so much less specie to India than they had obtained from Portugal. They would have brought to Europe and sold on the Continent just that much less of East Indian merchandise, and consequently would have taken home with them that much less of raw material.

Quite as untenable is Adam Smith's third argument that, if Portuguese money had not flowed in upon them, the English might have supplied their requirements of this article in other ways. Portugal, he conceived, must in any case have exported her superfluous store of precious metals, and these would have reached England through some other channel. We here assume that the Portuguese had manufactured their cloths for themselves, had themselves exported their superfluous stock of precious metals to India and China, and had purchased the return cargoes in other countries; and we take leave to ask the question whether under these circumstances the English would have seen much of Portuguese money? It would have been just the same if Portugal had concluded a Methuen Treaty with Holland or France. In both these cases, no doubt, some little of the money would have gone over to England, but only so much as she could have acquired by the sale of her raw wool. In short, but for the Methuen Treaty, the manufactures, the trade, and the shipping of the English could never have reached such a degree of expansion as they have attained to.

But whatever be the estimate formed of the effects of the Methuen Treaty as respects England, this much at least appears to be made out, that, in respect to Portugal, they have in no way been such as to tempt other nations to deliver over their home markets for manufactured goods to English competition, for the sake of facilitating the exportation of agricultural produce. Agriculture and trade, commerce and navigation, instead of improving from the intercourse with England, went on sinking lower and lower in Portugal. In vain did Pombal strive to raise them, English competition frustrated all his efforts. At the same time it must not be forgotten that in a country like Portugal, where the whole social conditions are opposed to progress in agriculture, industry, and commerce, commercial policy can effect but very little. Nevertheless, the little which Pombal did effect proves how much can be done for the benefit of industry by a government which is anxious to promote its interests, if only the internal hindrances which the social condition of a country presents can first be removed.

The same experience was made in Spain in the reigns of Philip V and his two immediate successors. Inadequate as was the protection extended to home industries under the Bourbons, and great as was the lack of energy in fully enforcing the customs laws, yet the remarkable animation which pervaded every branch of industry and every district of the country as the result of transplanting the commercial policy of Colbert from France to Spain was unmistakable.(12*) The statements of Ustaritz and Ulloa(13*) in regard to these results under the then prevailing circumstances are astonishing. For at that time were found everywhere only the most wretched mule-tracks, nowhere any well-kept inns, nowhere any bridges, canals, or river navigation, every province was closed against the rest of Spain by an internal customs cordon, at every city gate a royal toll was demanded, highway robbery and mendicancy were pursued as regular professions, the contraband trade was in the most flourishing condition, and the most grinding system of taxation existed; these and such as these the above named writers adduce as the causes of the decay of industry and agriculture.

The causes of these evils — fanaticism, the greed and the vices of the clergy, the privileges of the nobles, the despotism of the Government, the want of enlightenment and freedom amongst the people — Ustaritz and Ulloa dare not denounce.

A worthy counterpart to the Methuen Treaty with Portugal is the Assiento Treaty of 1713 with Spain, under which power was granted to the English to introduce each year a certain number of African negroes into Spanish America, and to visit the harbour of Portobello with one ship once a year, whereby an opportunity was afforded them of smuggling immense quantities of goods into these countries.

We thus find that in all treaties of commerce concluded by the English, there is a tendency to extend the sale of their manufactures throughout all the countries with whom they negotiate, by offering them apparent advantages in respect of agricultural produce and raw materials. Everywhere their efforts are directed to ruining the native manufacturing power of those countries by means of cheaper goods and long credits. If they cannot obtain low tariffs, then they devote their exertions to defrauding the custom-houses, and to organising a wholesale system of contraband trade. The former device, as we have seen, succeeded in Portugal, the latter in Spain. The collection of import dues upon the ad valorem principle has stood them in good stead in this matter, for which reason of late they have taken so much pains to represent the principle of paying duty by weight — as introduced by Prussia —as being injudicious.

NOTES:

1. Anderson, vol. i. p. 127, vol. ii. p. 350.

2. M. G. Simon, Recueil d'Observations sur l'Angleterre. Mémoires et Considérations sur le Commerce et les Finances d'Espagne. Ustaritz, Théorie et Pratique du Commerce.

3. Chaptal, De l'Industrie Française, vol. ii. p. 245.

4. The chief export trade of the Portuguese from Central and Southern America consisted of the precious metals. From 1748 to 1753, the exports amounted to 18 millions of piastres. See Humboldt's Essai Politique sur le Royaume de la Nouvelle Espagne, vol. ii. p. 652. The goods trade with those regions, as well as with the West Indies, first assumed important proportions, by the introduction of the sugar, coffee, and cotton planting.

5. British Merchant, vol. iii. p. 69.

6. Ibid. p. 71.

7. Ibid. p. 76.

8. Anderson, vol. iii. p. 67.

9. British Merchant, vol. iii. p. 267.

10. Ibid. vol. iii. pp. 15, 20, 33, 38, 110, 253, 254.

11. Anderson for the year 1703.

12. Macpherson, Annals of Commerce for the years 1771 and 1774. The obstacles thrown in the way of the importation of foreign goods greatly promoted the development of Spanish

manufactures. Before that time Spain had been obtaining nineteen-twentieths of her supplies of manufactured goods from England. — Brougham, Inquiry into the Colonial Policy of the European Powers, Part I. p. 421.

13. Ustaritz, Théorie du Commerce. Ulloa, Rétablissement des Manufactures d'Espagne.

Chapter 6

The French

France, too, inherited many a remnant of Roman Civilisation. On the irruption of the German Franks, who loved nothing but the chase, and changed many districts again into forests and waste which had been long under cultivation, almost everything was lost again. To the monasteries, however, which subsequently became such a great hindrance to civilisation, France, like all other European countries, is indebted for most of her progress in agriculture during the Middle Ages. The inmates of religious houses kept up no feuds like the nobles, nor harassed their vassals with calls to military service, while their lands and cattle were less exposed to rapine and extermination. The clergy loved good living, were averse to quarrels, and sought to gain reputation and respect by supporting the necessitous. Hence the old adage 'It is good to dwell under the crosier.' The Crusades, the institution of civic communities and of guilds by Louis IX (Saint Louis), and the proximity of Italy and Flanders, had considerable effect at an early period in developing industry in France. Already in the fourteenth century, Normandy and Brittany supplied woollen and linen cloths for home consumption and for export to England. At this period also the export trade in wines and salt, chiefly through the agency of Hanseatic middlemen, had become important.

By the influence of Francis I the silk manufacture was introduced into the South of France. Henry IV favoured this industry, as well as the manufacture of glass, linen, and woollens; Richelieu and Mazarin favoured the silk manufacto-ries, the velvet and woollen manufactures of Rouen and Sedan, as well as the fisheries and navigation.

On no country did the discovery of America produce more favourable effects than upon France. From Western France quantities of corn were sent to Spain. Many peasants migrated every year from the Pyrenean districts to the north-east of Spain in search of work. Great quantities of wine and salt were exported to the Spanish Netherlands, while the silks, the velvets, as also especially the articles of luxury of French manufacture, were sold in considerable quantities in the Neth-erlands, England, Spain, and Portugal. Owing to this cause a great deal of Spanish gold and silver got into circulation in France at an early period.

But the palmy days of French industry first commenced with Colbert.

At the time of Mazarin's death, neither manufacturing industry, commerce, navigation, nor the fisheries had attained to importance, while the financial condition of the country was at its worst.

Colbert had the courage to grapple single-handed with an undertaking which England could only bring to a successful issue by the persevering efforts of three centuries, and at the cost of two revolutions. From all countries he obtained the most skilful workmen, bought up trade secrets, and procured better machinery and tools. By a general and efficient tariff he secured the home markets for native industry. By abolishing, or by limiting as much as possible, the provincial customs collec-tions, by the construction of highways and canals, he promoted internal traffic. These measures benefited agriculture even more than manufacturing industry because the number of consumers was thereby doubled and trebled, and the producers were brought into easy and cheap communication with the consumers. He further promoted the interests of agriculture by lowering the amounts of direct imposts levied upon landed property, by mitigating the severity of the stringent measures previously adopted in collecting the revenue, by equalising the incidence of taxation, and lastly by introducing measures for the reduction of the rate of interest. He prohibited the exportation of corn only in times of scarcity and high prices. To the extension of the foreign trade and the promotion of fisheries he devoted special attention. He re-established the trade with the Levant, enlarged that with the colonies, and opened up a trade with the North. Into all branches of the administration he introduced the most stringent economy and perfect order. At his death France possessed 50,000 looms engaged in the manufacture of woollens; she produced annually silk manufactures to the value of 50 millions of francs. The State revenues had increased by 28 millions of francs. The kingdom was in possession of flourishing fisheries, of an extensive mercantile marine, and a powerful navy.(1*)

A century later, the economists have sharply censured Colbert, and maintained that this statesman had been anxious to promote the interests of manufactures at the expense of agriculture: a reproach which proves nothing more than that these authorities were themselves incapable of appreciating the nature of manufacturing industry.(2*)

If, however, Colbert was in error in opposing periodical obstacles to the exportation of raw materials, yet by fostering the growth and progress of native industries he so greatly increased the demand for agricultural produce that he gave the agricultural interest tenfold compensation for any injury which he caused to it by the above-named obstacles. If, contrary to the dictates of enlightened statesmanship, he prescribed new processes of manufacture, and compelled the manufacturers by penal enactments to adopt them, it should be borne in mind that these processes were the best and the most profitable known in his day, and that he had to deal with a people which, sunk into the utmost apathy by reason of a long despotic rule, resisted every innovation even though it was an improvement.

The reproach, however, that France had lost a large portion of her native industry through Colbert's protective system, could be levelled against Colbert only by that school which utterly ignored the revocation of the Edict of Nantes with its disastrous consequences. In consequence of these deplorable measures, in the course of three years after Colbert's death half a million of the most industrious, skilful, and thriving inhabitants of France were banished; who, consequently, to the double injury of France which they had enriched, transplanted their industry and their capital to Switzerland, to every Protestant country in Germany, especially to Prussia, as also to Holland and England. Thus the intrigues of a bigoted courtesan ruined in three years the able and gifted work of a whole generation, and cast France back again into its previous state of apathy; while England, under the aegis of her Constitution, and invigorated by a Revolution which called forth all the energies of the nation, was prosecuting with increasing ardour and without intermission the work commenced by Elizabeth and her predecessors.

The melancholy condition to which the industry and the finances of France had been reduced by a long course of misgovernment, and the spectacle of the great prosperity of England, aroused the emulation of French statesmen shortly before the French Revolution. Infatuated with the hollow theory of the economists, they looked for a remedy, in opposition to Colbert's policy, in the establishment of free trade. It was thought that the prosperity of the country could be restored at one blow if a better market were provided for French wines and brandies in England, at the cost of permitting the importation of English manufactures upon easy terms (a twelve per cent duty). England, delighted at the proposal, willingly granted to the French a second edition of the Methuen Treaty, in the shape of the so-called Eden Treaty of 1786; a copy which was soon followed by results not less ruinous than those produced by the Portuguese original.

The English, accustomed to the strong wines of the Peninsula, did not increase their consumption to the extent which had been expected, whilst the French perceived with horror that all they had to offer the English were simply fashions and fancy articles, the total value of which was insignificant : whereas the English manufacturers, in all articles of prime necessity, the total amount of which was enormous, could greatly surpass the French manufacturers in cheapness of prices, as well as in quality of their goods, and in granting of credit. When, after a brief competition, the French manufacturers were brought to the brink of ruin, while French wine-growers had gained but little, then the French Government sought to arrest the progress of this ruin by terminating the treaty, but only acquired the conviction that it is much easier to ruin flourishing manufactories in a few years than to revive ruined manufactories in a whole generation. English competition had engendered a taste for English goods in France, the consequence of which was an extensive and long-continued contraband trade which it was difficult to suppress. Meanwhile it was not so difficult for the English, after the termination of the treaty, to accustom their palates again to the wines of the Peninsula.

Notwithstanding that the commotions of the Revolution and the incessant wars of Napoleon could not have been favourable to the prosperity of French industry notwithstanding that the French lost during this period most of their maritime trade and all their colonies, yet French manufactories, solely from their exclusive possession of their home markets, and from the abrogation of feudal restrictions, attained during the Empire to a higher degree of prosperity than they had ever enjoyed under the preceding ancien régime. The same effects were noticeable in Germany and in all countries over which the Continental blockade extended.

Napoleon said in his trenchant style, that under the existing circumstances of the world any State which adopted the principle of free trade must come to the ground. In these words he uttered more political wisdom in reference to the commercial policy of France than all contemporary political economists in all their writings. We cannot but wonder at the sagacity with which this great genius, without any previous study of the systems of political economy, comprehended the nature and importance of manufacturing power. Well was it for him and for France that he had not studied these systems. 'Formerly,' said Napoleon, 'there was but one description of property, the possession of land; but a new property has now risen up, namely, industry.' Napoleon saw, and in this way clearly enunciated, what contemporary economists did not see, or did not clearly enunciate, namely, that a nation which combines in itself the power of manufactures with that of agriculture is an immeasurably more perfect and more wealthy nation than a purely agricultural one. What Napoleon did to found and promote the industrial education of France, to improve the country's credit, to introduce and set going new inventions and improved processes, and to perfect the means of internal communication in France, it is not necessary to dwell upon in detail, for these things are still too well remembered. But what, perhaps, does call for special notice in this connection, is the biassed and unfair judgment passed upon this enlightened and powerful ruler by contemporary theorists.

With the fall of Napoleon, English competition, which had been till then restricted to a contraband trade, recovered its footing on the continents of Europe and America. Now for the first time the English were heard to condemn protection and to eulogise Adam Smith's doctrine of free trade, a doctrine which heretofore those practical islanders considered as suited only to an ideal state of Utopian perfection. But an impartial, critical observer might easily discern the entire aBsence of mere sentimental motives of philanthropy in this conversion, for only when increased facilities for the exportation of English goods to the continents of Europe and America were in question were cosmopolitan arguments resorted to; but so soon as the question turned upon the free importation of corn, or whether foreign goods might be allowed to compete at all with British manufactures in the English market, in that case quite different principles were appealed to.(3*) Unhappily, it was said, the long continuance in England of a policy contrary to natural principles had created an artificial state of things, which could not Be interfered with suddenly without incurring the risk of dangerous and mischievous consequences. It was not to be attempted without the greatest caution and prudence. It was England's misfortune, not her fault. All the more gratifying ought it to be for the nations of the European and American continents, that their happy lot and condition left them quite free to partake without delay of the blessings of free trade.

In France, although her ancient dynasty reascended the throne under the protection of the banner of England, or at any rate by the influence of English gold, the above arguments did not obtain currency for very long. England's free trade wrought

92

such havoc amongst the manufacturing industries which had prospered and grown strong under the Continental blockade system, that a prohibitive régime was speedily resorted to, under the protecting aegis of which, according to Dupin's testimony,(4*) the producing power of French manufactories was doubled between the years 1815 and 1827.

NOTES:

1. 'Eloge de Jean Baptiste Colbert, par Necker' (1773) (OEuvres Completes, vol. xv.).

2. See Quesnay's paper entitled, 'Physiocratie, ou du Gouvernement le plus avantageux au Genre Humain (1768),' Note 5, 'sur la maxime viii,' wherein Quesnay contradicts and condemns Colbert in two brief pages, whereas Necker devoted a hundred pages to the exposition of Colbert's system and of what he accomplished. It is hard to say whether we are to wonder most at the ignorance of Quesnay on matters of industry, history, and finance, or at the presumption with which he passes judgment upon such a man as Colbert without adducing grounds for it. Add to that, that this ignorant dreamer was not even candid enough to mention the expulsion of the Huguenots; nay, that he was not ashamed to allege, contrary to all truth, that Colbert had restricted the trade in corn between province and province by vexatious police ordinances.

3. A highly accomplished American orator, Mr Baldwin, Chief Justice of the United States, when referring to the Canning-Huskisson system of free trade, shrewdly remarked, that, like most English productions, it had been manufactured not so much for home consumption as for exportation.

Shall we laugh most or weep when we call to mind the rapture of enthusiasm with which the Liberals in France and Germany, more particularly the cosmopolitan theorists of the philanthropic school, and notably Mons. J. B. Say, hailed the announcement of the Canning-Huskisson system? So great was their jubilation, that one might have thought the millennium had come. But let us see what Mr Canning's own biographer says about this minister's views on the subject of free trade.

'Mr Canning was perfectly convinced of the truth of the abstract principle, that commerce is sure to flourish most when wholly unfettered; but since such had not been the opinion either of our ancestors or of surrounding nations, and since in consequence restraints had been imposed upon all commercial transactions, a state of things had grown up to which the unguarded application of the abstract principle, however true it was in theory, might have been somewhat mischievous in practice.' (The Political Life of Mr Canning, by Stapleton, p. 3.) In the year 1828, these same tactics of the English had again assumed a prominence so marked that Mr Hume, the Liberal member of Parliament, felt no hesitation in stigmatising them in the House as the strangling of Continental industries.

4. Forces productives de la France.

Chapter 7

The Germans

In the chapter on the Hanseatic League we saw how; next in order to Italy, Germany had flourished, through extensive commerce, long before the other European states. We have now to continue the industrial history of that nation, after first taking a rapid survey of its earliest industrial circumstances and their development.

In ancient Germania, the greater part of the land was devoted to pasturage and parks for game. The insignificant and primitive agriculture was abandoned to serfs and to women. The sole occupation of the freemen was warfare and the chase; and that is the origin of all the German nobility.

The German nobles firmly adhered to this system throughout the Middle Ages, oppressing agriculturists and opposing manufacturing industry, while quite blind to the benefits which must accrued to them, as the lords of the soil, from the prosperity of both.

Indeed, so deeply rooted has the passion for their hereditary favourite occupation ever continued with the German nobles, that even in the our days, long after they have been enriched by the ploughshare and shuttle, they still dream in legislative the about the preservation of game and the game laws, as though the wolf and the sheep, the bear and the bee, could dwell in peace side by side; as though landed property could be devoted at one and the same time to gardening, timber growing, and scientific farming, and to the preservation of wild boars, deer, and hares.

German husbandry long remained in a barbarous condition, notwithstanding that the influence of towns and monasteries on the districts in their immediate vicinity could not be ignored.

Towns sprang up in the ancient Roman colonies, at the seats of the temporal and ecclesiastical princes and lords, near monasteries, and, where favoured by the Emperor, to a certain extent within their domains and inclosures, also on sites where the fisheries, combined with facilities for land and water transport, offered inducements to them. They flourished in most cases only by supplying the local requirements, and by the foreign transport trade. An extensive system of native industry capable Of supplying an export trade could only have grown up by means of extensive sheep farming and extensive cultivation of flax. But flax cultivation implies a high standard of agriculture, while extensive sheep farming needs protection against wolves and robbers. Such protection could not be maintained amid the perpetual feuds of the nobles and princes between themselves and against the towns. Cattle pastures served always as the principal field for robbery; while the total extermination of beasts of prey was out of the question with those vast tracts of forest which the nobility so carefully preserved for their indulgence in the chase. The scanty number of cattle, the insecurity of life and property, the entire lack of capital and of freedom on the part of the cultivators of the soil, or of any interest in agriculture on the part of those who owned it, necessarily tended to keep agriculture, and with it the prosperity of the towns, in a very low state.

If these circumstances are duly considered, it is easy to understand the reason why Flanders and Brabant under totally opposite conditions attained at so early a period to a high degree of liberty and prosperity.

Notwithstanding these impediments, the German cities on

the Baltic and the German Ocean flourished, owing to the fisheries, to navigation, and the foreign trade at sea; in Southern Germany and at the foot of the Alps, owing to the influence of Italy, Greece, and the transport trade by land; on the Rhine, the Elbe, and the Danube, by means of viticulture and the wine trade, owing to the exceptional fertility of the soil and the facilities of water communication, which in the Middle Ages was of still greater importance than even in our days, because of the wretched condition of the roads and the general state of insecurity.

This diversity of origin will explain the diversity characterising the several confederations of German cities, such as the Hanseatic, the Rhenish, the Swabian, the Dutch, and the Helvetic.

Though they continued powerful for a time owing to the spirit of youthful freedom which pervaded them, yet these leagues lacked the internal guarantee of stability, the principle of unity, the cement. Separated from each other by the estates of the nobility, by the serfdom of the population of the country, their union was doomed sooner or later to break down, owing to the gradual increase and enrichment of the agricultural population, among whom, through the power of the princes, the principle of unity was maintained. The cities, inasmuch as they tended to promote the prosperity of agriculture, by so doing necessarily were working at their own effacement, unless they contrived to incorporate the agricultural classes or the nobility as members of their unions. For the accomplishment of that object, however, they lacked the requisite higher political instincts and knowledge. Their political vision seldom extended beyond their own city walls.

Two only of these confederations, Switzerland and the Seven United Provinces, actually carried out this incorporation, and that not as the result of reflection, but because they were compelled to it, and favoured by circumstances, and for that reason those confederations still exist. The Swiss Confederation is nothing but a conglomerate of German imperial cities, established and cemented together by the free populations occupying the intervening tracts of country.

The remaining leagues of German cities were ruined owing to their contempt for the rural population, and from their absurd burgher arrogance, which delighted in keeping that population in subjection, rather than in raising them to their own level.

These cities could only have attained unity by means of an hereditary royal authority. But this authority in Germany lay in the hands of the princes, who, in order to avert restraints upon their own arbitrary rule, and to keep both the cities and the minor nobles in subjection, were interested in resisting the establishment of an hereditary empire.

Hence the persevering adherence to the idea of the Imperial Roman Empire amongst German kings. Only at the head of armies were the emperors rulers; only when they went to war were they able to bring together princes and cities under their banner. Hence their protection of civic liberty in Germany, and their hostility to it and persecution of it in Italy.

The expeditions to Rome not only weakened more and more the kingly power in Germany, they weakened those very dynasties through which, within the Empire, in the heart of the nation, a consolidated power might have grown up. But with the extinction of the House of Hohenstaufen the nucleus of consolidated power was broken up into a thousand fragments.

The sense of the impossibility of consolidating the heart of the nation impelled the House of Hapsburg, originally so weak and poor, to utilise the nation's vigour in founding a consolidated hereditary monarchy on the south-eastern frontier of the

German Empire, by subjugating alien races, a policy which in the northeast was imitated by the Margraves of Brandenburg. Thus in the south-east and north-east there arose hereditary sovereignties founded upon the dominion over alien races, while in the two western corners of the land two republics grew into existence which continually separated themselves more and more from the parent nation; and within, in the nation's heart, disintegration, impotence, and dissolution continually progressed. The misfortunes of the German nation were completed by the inventions of gunpowder and of the art of printing, the revival of the Roman law, the Reformation, and lastly the discovery of America and of the new route to India.

The intellectual, social, and economic revolution which we have described produced divisions and disruption between the constituent members of the Empire, disunion between the princes, disunion between the cities, disunion even between the various guilds of individual cities, and between neighbours of every rank. The energies of the nation were now diverted from the pursuit of industry, agriculture, trade, and navigation; from the acquisition of colonies, the amelioration of internal institutions, in fact from every kind of substantial improvement, the people contended about dogmas and the heritage of the Church.

At the same time came the decline of the Hanseatic League and of Venice, and with it the decline of Germany's wholesale trade, and of the power and liberties of the German cities both in the north and in the south.

Then came the Thirty Years' War with its devastations of all territories and cities. Holland and Switzerland seceded, while the fairest provinces of the Empire were conquered by France. Whereas formerly single cities, such as Strasburg, Nürnberg, Augsburg, had surpassed in power entire electorates, they now sank into utter impotence in consequence of the introduction of

99

standing armies.

If before this revolution the cities and the royal power had been more consolidated — if a king exclusively belonging to the German nation had obtained a complete mastery of the Reformation, and had carried it out in the interests of the unity, power, and freedom of the nation — how very differently would the agriculture, industry, and trade of the Germans have been developed. By the side of considerations such as these, how pitiable and unpractical seems that theory of political economy which would have us refer the material welfare of nations solely to the production of individuals, wholly losing sight of the fact that the producing power of all individuals is to a great extent determined by the social and political circumstances of the nation. The introduction of the Roman law weakened no nation so much as the German. The unspeakable confusion which it brought into the legal status and relations of private individuals, was not the worst of its bad effects. More mischievous was it by far, in that it created a caste of learned men and jurists differing from the people in spirit and language, which treated the people as a class unlearned in the law, as minors, which denied the authority of all sound human understanding, which everywhere set up secrecy in the room of publicity, which, living in the most abject dependence and living upon arbitrary power, everywhere advocated it and defended its interests, everywhere gnawed at the roots of liberty. Thus we see even to the beginning of the eighteenth century in Germany, barbarism in literature and language, barbarism in legislation, State administration and administration of justice; barbarism in agriculture, decline of industry and of all trade upon a large scale, want of unity and of force in national cohesion; powerlessness and weakness on all hands in dealing with foreign nations.

One thing only the Germans had preserved; that was their aboriginal character, their love of industry, order, thrift, and moderation, their perseverance and endurance in research and in business, their honest striving after improvement, and a considerable natural measure of morality, prudence, and circumspection.

This character both the rulers and the ruled had in common. After the almost total decay of nationality and the restoration of tranquillity, people began in some individual isolated circles to introduce order, improvement, and progress. Nowhere was witnessed more zeal in cherishing education, manners, religion, art, and science; nowhere was absolute power exercised with greater moderation or with more advantage to general enlightenment, order, and morality, to the reform of abuses and the advancement of the common welfare.

The foundation for the revival of German nationality was undoubtedly laid by the Governments them selves, by their conscientious devotion of the proceeds of the secularised Church lands to the uses of education and instruction, of art and science, of morality and objects of public utility. By these measures light made its way into the State administration and the administration of justice, into education and literature, into agriculture, industry, and commerce, and above all amongst the masses. Thus Germany developed herself in a totally different way from all other nations. Elsewhere high mental culture rather grew out of the evolution of the material powers of production, whilst in Germany the growth of material powers of production was the outcome chiefly of an antecedent intellectual development. Hence at the present day the whole culture of the Germans is theoretical. Hence also those many unpractical and odd traits in the German character which other nations notice in us.

For the moment the Germans are in the position of an individual who, having been formerly deprived of the use of his limbs, first learned theoretically the arts of standing and walking, of eating and drinking, of laughing and weeping, and then only proceeded to put them in practice. Hence comes the German predilection for philosophic systems and cosmopolitan dreams. The intellect, which was not allowed to stir in the affairs of this world, strove to exercise itself in the realms of speculation. Hence, too, we find that nowhere has the doctrine of Adam Smith and of his disciples obtained a larger following than in Germany; nowhere else have people more thoroughly believed in the cosmopolitan magnanimity of Messrs Canning and Huskisson.

For the first progress in manufactures Germany is indebted to the revocation of the Edict of Nantes and to the numerous refugees who by that insane measure were driven to emigrate to almost every part of Germany, and established everywhere manufactures of wool, silk, jewellery, hats, glass, china, gloves, and industries of every kind.

The first Government measures for the promotion of manufactures in Germany were introduced by Austria and Prussia; in Austria under Charles VI and Maria Theresa, but even more under Joseph II. Austria had formerly suffered enormously from the banishment of the Protestants, her most industrious citizens; nor can it be exactly affirmed that she distinguished herself in the immediate sequel by promoting enlightenment and mental culture. Afterwards, in consequence of a protective tariff, improved sheep farming, better roads, and other encouragements, industry made considerable strides even under Maria Theresa.

More energetically still was this work pushed forward under Joseph II and with immensely greater success. At first, indeed, the results could not be called important, because the Emperor, according to his wont, was too precipitate in these as in all his other schemes of reform, and Austria, in relation to other states, still occupied too backward a position. Here as elsewhere it became evident that one might get 'too much of a good thing' at once, and that protective duties, in order to work beneficially and not as a disturbing element upon an existing state of things, must not be made too high at the commencement. But the longer that system continued, the more clearly was its wisdom demonstrated. To that tariff Austria is indebted for her present prosperous industries and the flourishing condition of her agriculture.

The industry of Prussia had suffered more than that of any other country from the devastations of the Thirty Years' War. Her most important industry, the manufacture of cloth in the Margravate of Brandenburg, was almost entirely annihilated. The majority of cloth workers had migrated to Saxony, while English imports at the time held every competition in check. To the advantage of Prussia now came the revocation of the Edict of Nantes and the persecution of the Protestants in the Palatinate and in Salzburg. The great Elector saw at a glance what Elizabeth before him had so clearly understood. In consequence of the measures devised by him a great number of the fugitives directed their steps to Prussia, fertilised the agricultural industry of the land, established a large number of manufactures, and cultivated science and art. All his successors followed in his footsteps, none with more zeal than the great King — greater by his policy in times of peace than by his successes in war. Space is wanting to treat at length of the countless measures whereby Frederick II attracted to his dominions large numbers of foreign agriculturists, brought tracts of waste land into cultivation, and established the cultivation of meadows, of cattle fodder, vegetables, potatoes, and tobacco, improved sheep farming, cattle breeding, horse breeding, the use of mineral manures, &c., by which means he created capital and credit for the benefit of the agricultural classes. Still more than by these direct measures he promoted indirectly the interests of agriculture by means of those branches of manufacture which, in consequence of the customs tariff and the improved means of transport which he established, as well as the establishment of a bank, made greater advances in Prussia than in any other German state, notwithstanding that that country's geographical position, and its division into several provinces separated from one another, were much less favourable for the success of such measures, and that the disadvantages of a customs cordon, namely, the damaging effects of a contraband trade, must be felt more acutely there than in great states whose territories are compact and well protected by boundaries of seas, rivers, and chains of mountains.

At the same time we are nowise anxious, under cover of this eulogy, to defend the faults of the system, such as, for example, the restrictions laid upon the exportation of raw material. Still, that in despite of these faults the national industry was considerably advanced by it, no enlightened and impartial historian would venture to dispute.

To every unprejudiced mind, unclouded by false theories, it must be clear that Prussia gained her title to rank amongst the European powers not so much by her conquests as by her wise policy in promoting the interests of agriculture, industry, and trade, and by her progress in literature and science; and all this was the work of one great genius alone.

And yet the Crown was not yet supported by the energy of free institutions, but simply by an administrative system, well ordered and conscientious, but unquestionably trammelled by the dead mechanical routine of a hierarchical bureaucracy.

Meanwhile all the rest of Germany had for centuries been under the influence of free trade — that is to say, the whole world was free to export manufactured products into Germany, while no one consented to admit German manufactured goods into other countries. This rule had its exceptions, but only a few. It cannot, however, be asserted that the predictions and the promises of the school about the great benefits of free trade have been verified by the experience of this country, for everywhere the movement was rather retrograde than progressive. Cities like Augsburg, Nürnberg, Mayence, Cologne, &c., numbered no more than a third or a fourth part of their former population, and wars were often wished for merely for the sake of getting rid of a valueless surplus of produce.

The wars came in the train of the French Revolution, and with them English subsidies together with increased English competition. Hence a new downward tendency in manufactures coupled with an increase in agricultural prosperity, which, however, was only apparent and transitory.

Next followed Napoleon's Continental Blockade, an event which marked an era in the history of both German and French industry, notwithstanding that Mons. J. B. Say, Adam Smith's most famous pupil, denounced it as a calamity. Whatever theorists, and notably the English, may urge against it, this much is clearly made out —and all who are conversant with German industry must attest it, for there is abundant evidence of the fact in all statistical writings of that day — that, as a result of this blockade, German manufactures of all and every kind for the first time began to make an important advance;(1*) that then only did the improved breeding of sheep (which had been commenced some time before) become general and successful; that then only was activity displayed in improving

105

the means of transport. It is true, on the other hand, that Germany lost the greater part of her former export trade, especially in linens. Yet the gain was considerably greater than the loss, particularly for the Prussian and Austrian manufacturing establishments, which had previously gained a start over all other manufactories in the German states.

But with the return of peace the English manufacturers again entered into a fearful competition with the German; for during the reciprocal blockade, in consequence of new inventions and a great and almost exclusive export trade to foreign lands, the manufactories of the island had far outstripped that of Germany; and for this reason, as well as because of their large acquired capital, the former were first in a position to sell at much lower prices, to offer much superior articles, and to give much longer credit than the latter, which had still to battle with the difficulties of a first beginning. Consequently general ruin followed and loud wailings amongst the latter, especially in the lower Rhenish provinces, in those regions which, having formerly belonged to France, were now excluded from the French market. Besides, the Prussian customs tariff had undergone many changes in the direction of absolute free trade, and no longer afforded any sufficient protection against English competition. At the same time the Prussian bureaucracy long strove against the country's cry for help. They had become too strongly imbued with Adam Smith's theory at the universities to discern the want of the times with sufficient promptness. There even still existed political economists in Prussia who harboured the bold design of reviving the long-exploded 'physiocratic' system. Meanwhile the nature of things here too proved a mightier force than the power of theories. The cry of distress raised by the manufacturers, hailing as it did from districts still yearning after their former state of connection with France, whose sympathies it was necessary to conciliate, could not be safely disregarded too long. More and more the opinion spread at the time that the English Government were favouring in an unprecedented manner a scheme for glutting the markets on the Continent with manufactured goods in order to stifle the Continental manufactures in the cradle. This idea has been ridiculed, but it was natural enough that it should prevail, first, because this glutting really took place in such a manner as though it had been deliberately planned; and, secondly, because a celebrated member of Parliament, Mr Henry Brougham (afterwards Lord Brougham), had openly said, in 1815, 'that it was well worth while to incur a loss on the exportation of English manufactures in order to stifle in the cradle the foreign manufactures.'(2*) This idea of this lord, since so renowned as a philanthropist, cosmopolist, and Liberal, was repeated ten years later almost in the same words by Mr Hume, a member of Parliament not less distinguished for liberalism, when he expressed a wish that 'Continental manufactures might be nipped in the bud.'

At length the prayer of the Prussian manufacturers found a hearing — late enough, indeed, as must be admitted when one considers how painful it is to be wrestling with death year after year — but at last their cry was heard to real good purpose. The Prussian customs tariff of 1818 answered, for the time in which it was established, all the requirements of Prussian industry, without in any way overdoing the principle of protection or unduly interfering with the country's beneficial intercourse with foreign countries. Its scale of duties was much lower than those of the English and French customs systems, and necessarily so; for in this case there was no question of a gradual transition from a prohibitive to a protective system, but of a change from free trade (so called) to a protective system. Another great advantage of this tariff, considered as a whole, was that the duties were mostly levied according to the weight of goods and not according to their value. By this means not only were smuggling and too low valuations obviated, but also the great object was gained, that articles of general consumption, which every country can most easily manufacture for itself, and the manufacture of which, because of their great total money value, is the most important of any for the country, were burdened with the highest import duty, while the protective duty fell lower and lower in proportion to the fineness and costliness of the goods, also as the difficulty of making such articles at home increased, and also as both the inducements and the facilities for smuggling increased.

But this mode of charging the duty upon the weight would of course, for very obvious reasons, affect the trade with the neighbouring German states much more injuriously than the trade with foreign nations. The second-rate and smaller German states had now to bear, in addition to their exclusion from the Austrian, French, and English markets, almost total exclusion from that of Prussia, which hit them all the harder, since many of them were either totally or in great part hemmed in by Prussian provinces.

Just in proportion as these measures pacified the Prussian manufacturers, was the loudness of the outcry against them on the part of the manufacturers of the other German states. Add to that, that Austria had shortly before imposed restrictions on the importation of German goods into Italy, notably of the linens of Upper Swabia. Restricted on all sides in their export trade to small strips of territory, and further being separated from one another by smaller internal lines of customs duties, the manufacturers of these countries were well-nigh in despair.

It was this state of urgent necessity which led to the formation of that private union of five to six thousand German manufacturers and merchants, which was founded in the year 1819 at the spring fair held in Frankfort-on-the-Main, with the object of abolishing all the separate tariffs of the various German states, and on the other hand of establishing a common trade and custom-house system for the whole of Germany.

This union was formally organised. Its articles of association were submitted to the Diet, and to all the rulers and governments of the German states for approval. In every German town a local correspondent was appointed; each German state had its provincial correspondent. All the members and correspondents bound themselves to promote the objects of the union to the best of their ability. The city of Nürnberg was selected as the head-quarters of the union, and authorised to appoint a central committee, which should direct the business of the union, under the advice of an assessor, for which office the author of this book was selected. In a weekly journal of the union, bearing the title of 'Organ des deutschen Handels- und Fabrikantenstandes,'(3*) the transactions and measures of the central committee were made known, and ideas, proposals, treatises, and statistical papers relating to the objects of the union were published. Each year at the spring fair in Frankfort a general meeting of the union was held, at which the central committee gave an account of its stewardship.

After this union had presented a petition to the German Diet showing the need and expediency of the measures proposed by their organisation, the central committee at Nürnberg commenced operations. Deputations were sent to every German Court, and finally one to the Congress of Plenipotentiaries held at Vienna in 1820. At this congress so much at least was gained, that several of the second-class and smaller German states agreed to hold a separate congress on the subject at

Darmstadt. The effect of the deliberations of this last-named congress was, first, to bring about a union between Würtemberg and Bavaria; secondly, a union of some of the German states and Prussia; then a union between the middle German states; lastly, and chiefly in consequence of the exertions of Freiherr von Cotta to fuse the above-named three unions into a general customs confederation, so that at this present time, with the exception of Austria, the two Mecklenburgs, Hanover, and the Hanse Towns, the whole of Germany is associated in a single customs union, which has abolished the separate customs lines amongst its members, and has established a uniform tariff in common against the foreigner, the revenue derived from which is distributed pro rata amongst the several states according to their populations.

The tariff of this union is substantially the same as that established by Prussia in 1818; that is to say, it is a moderate protectionist tariff.

In consequence of this unification of customs, the industry, trade, and agriculture of the German states forming the union have already made enormous strides.

NOTES:

1. The system must necessarily have affected France in a different manner than Germany, because Germany was mostly shut out from the French markets, while the German markets were all open to the French manufacturer.

2. Report of the Committee of Commerce and Manufactures to the House of Representatives of the Congress of the United States, Feb. 13, 1816.

3. Organ of the German Commercial and Manufacturing Interests.

Chapter 8

The Russians

Russia owes her first progress in civilisation and industry to her intercourse with Greece, to the trade of the Hanseatic Towns with Novgorod and (after the destruction of that town by Ivan Wassiljewitsch) to the trade which arose with the English and Dutch, in consequence of the discovery of the water communication with the coasts of the White Sea.

But the great increase of her industry, and especially of her civilisation, dates from the reign of Peter the Great. The history of Russia during the last hundred and forty years offers a most striking proof of the great influence of national unity and political circumstances on the economic welfare of a nation.

To the imperial power which established and maintained this union of innumerable Barbaric hordes, Russia owes the foundations of her manufactures, her vast progress in agriculture and population, the facilities offered to her interior traffic by the construction of canals and roads, a very large foreign trade, and her standing as a commercial power.

Russia's independent system of trade dates, however, only from the year 1821.

Under Catherine II. trade and manufactures had certainly made some progress, on account of the privileges she offered to foreign artisans and manufacturers; but the culture of the nation was still too imperfect to allow of its getting beyond the first stages in the manufacture of iron, glass, linen, &c., and especially in those branches of industry in which the country was specially favoured by its agricultural and mineral wealth.

Besides this, further progress in manufactures would not, at that time, have been conducive to the economic interests of the nation. If foreign countries had taken in payment the provisions, raw material, and rude manufactures which Russia was able to furnish if, further, no wars and exterior events had intervened, Russia by means of intercourse with nations more advanced than herself would have been much more prosperous, and her culture in general would in consequence of this intercourse have made greater progress than under the manufacturing system. But wars and the Continental blockade, and the commercial regulations of foreign nations, compelled her to seek prosperity in other ways than by the export of raw materials and the import of manufactures. In consequence of these, the previous commercial relations of Russia by sea were disturbed. Her overland trade with the western continent could not make up for these losses; and she found it necessary, therefore, to work up her raw materials herself. After the establishiment of the general peace, a desire arose to return to the old system. The Government, and even the Emperor, were inclined to favour free trade. In Russia, the writings of Herr Storch enjoyed as high a reputation as those of Mons Say in Germany. People were not alarmed by the first shocks which the home manufactories, which had arisen during the Continental Blockade, suffered owing to English competition. The theorists maintained that if these shocks could only be endured once for all, the blessings of free trade would follow. And indeed the circumstances of the commercial world at the time were uncommonly favourable to this transition. The failure of crops in Western Europe caused a great export of agricultural produce, by which Russia for a long time gained ample means to balance her large importation of manufactured goods.

But when this extraordinary demand for Russian agricultural

produce had ceased, when, on the other hand, England had imposed restrictions on the import of corn for the benefit of her aristocracy, and on that of foreign timber for the benefit of Canada, the ruin of Russia's home manufactories and the excessive import of foreign manufactures made itself doubly felt. Although people had formerly, with Herr Storch, considered the balance of trade as a chimera, to believe in the existence of which was, for a reasonable and enlightened man, no less outrageous and ridiculous than the belief in witchcraft in the seventeenth century had been, it was now seen with alarm that there must be something of the nature of a balance of trade as between independent nations. The most enlightened and discerning statesman of Russia, Count Nesselrode, did not hesitate to confess to this belief. He declared in an official circular of 1821: 'Russia finds herself compelled by circumstances to take up an independent system of trade; the products of the empire have found no foreign market, the home manufactures are ruined or on the point of being so, all the ready money of the country flows towards foreign lands, and the most substantial trading firms are nearly ruined.' The beneficial effects of the Russian protective system contributed no less than the injurious consequences of the re-establishment of free trade had done to bring into discredit the principles and assertions of the theorists. Foreign capital, talent, and labour flowed into the country from all civilised lands, especially from England and Germany, in order to share in the advantages offered by the home manufactories.

The nobility imitated the policy of the Empire at large. As they could obtain no foreign market for their produce, they attempted to solve the problem inversely by bringing the market into proximity with the produce — they established manufactories on their estates. In consequence of the demand

for fine wool produced by the newly created woollen manufactories, the breed of sheep was rapidly improved. Foreign trade
increased, instead of declining, particularly that with China,
Persia, and other neighbouring countries of Asia. The commercial crises entirely ceased, and one need only read the latest
reports of the Russian Minister of Commerce to be convinced
that Russia owes a large measure of prosperity to this system,
and that she is increasing her national wealth and power by
enormous strides.

It is foolish for Germans to try to make little of this progress
and to complain of the injury which it has caused to the north-
eastern provinces of Germany. Each nation, like each individual, has its own interests nearest at heart. Russia is not
called upon to care for the welfare of Germany; Germany must
care for Germany, and Russia for Russia. It would be much
better, instead of complaining, instead of hoping and waiting
and expecting the Messiah of a future free trade, to throw the
cosmopolitan system into the fire and take a lesson from the
example of Russia.

That England should look with jealousy on this commercial
policy of Russia is very natural. By its means Russia has
emancipated herself from England, and has qualified herself to
enter into competition with her in Asia. Even if England manufactures more cheaply, this advantage will in the trade with
Central Asia be outweighed by the proximity of the Russian
Empire and by its political influence. Although Russia may still
be, in comparison with Europe, but a slightly civilised country,
yet, as compared with Asia, she is a civilised one.

Meantime, it cannot be denied that the want of civilisation
and political institutions will greatly hinder Russia in her
further industrial and commercial progress, especially if the
Imperial Government does not succeed in harmonising her

115

political conditions with the requirements of industry, by the introduction of efficient municipal and provincial constitutions, by the gradual limitation and final abolition of serfdom, by the formation of an educated middle class and a free peasant class, and by the completion of means of internal transport and of communication with Central Asia. These are the conquests to which Russia is called in the present century, and on them depends her further progress in agriculture and industry, in trade, navigation and naval power. But in order to render reforms of this kind possible and practicable, the Russian aristocracy must first learn to feel that their own material interests will be most promoted by them.

Chapter 9

The North Americans

After our historical examination of the commercial policy of the European nations, with the exception of those from which there is nothing of importance to be learnt, we will cast a glance beyond the Atlantic Ocean at a people of colonists which has been raising itself almost before our eyes from the condition of entire dependence on the mother country, and of separation into a number of colonial provinces having no kind of political union between themselves, to that of a united, well-organised, free, powerful, industrious, rich, and independent nation, which will perhaps in the time of our grandchildren exalt itself to the rank of the first naval and commercial power in the world. The history of the trade and industry of North America is more instructive for our subject than any other can be, Because here the course of development proceeds rapidly, the periods of free trade and protection follow closely on each other, their consequences stand out clearly and sharply defined, and the whole machinery of national industry and State administration moves exposed before the eyes of the spectator.

The North American colonies were kept, in respect of trade and industry, in such complete thraldom by the mother country, that no sort of manufacture was permitted to them beyond domestic manufacture and the ordinary handicrafts. So late as the year 1750 a hat manufactory in the State of Massachusetts created so great sensation and jealousy in Parliament, that it declared all kinds of manufactories to be 'common nuisances,' not excepting iron works, notwithstanding that the country possessed in the greatest abundance all the requisite materials for the manufacture of iron. Even more recently, namely, in 1770, the great Chatham, made uneasy by the first manufacturing attempts of the New Englanders, declared that the colonies should not be permitted to manufacture so much as a horseshoe nail.

To Adam Smith belongs the merit of having first pointed out the injustice of this policy.

The monopoly of all manufacturing industry by the mother country was one of the chief causes of the American Revolution; the tea duty merely afforded an opportunity for its outbreak.

Freed from restrictions, in possession of all material and intellectual resources for manufacturing work, and separated from that nation from which they had previously been supplied with manufactured goods, and to which they had been selling their produce, and thus thrown with all their wants upon their own resources: manufactures of every kind in the North American free states received a mighty stimulus during the war of revolution, which in its turn had the effect of benefiting agriculture to such an extent that, notwithstanding the burdens and the devastation consequent upon the then recent war, the value of land and the rate of wages in these states everywhere rose immensely but as, after the peace of Paris, the faulty constitution of the free states made the introduction of a united commercial system impossible, and consequently English manufactured goods again obtained free admission, competition with which the newly established American manufactories had not strength enough to bear, the prosperity which had arisen during the war vanished much more quickly than it had grown up. An orator in Congress said afterwards of this crisis: 'We did buy, according to the advice of modem theorists, where we could buy cheapest, and our markets were flooded with foreign goods; English goods sold cheaper in our seaport towns than in Liverpool or London. Our manufacturers were being ruined; our merchants, even those who thought to enrich themselves by importation, became bankrupt; and all these causes together were so detrimental to agriculture, that landed property became very generally worthless, and consequently bankruptcy became general even among our landowners.'

This condition of things was by no means temporary; it lasted from the peace of Paris until the establishment of the federal constitution, and contributed more than any other circumstance to bring about a more intimate union between the free states and to impel them to give to Congress full powers for the maintenance of a united commercial policy. Congress was inundated with petitions from all the states — New York and South Carolina not excepted —in favour of protective measures for internal industry; and Washington, on the day of his inauguration, wore a suit of home-manufactured cloth, 'in order,' said a contemporary New York journal, 'in the simple and impressive manner so peculiar to this great man, to give to all his successors in office and to all future legislators a memorable lesson upon the way in which the welfare of this country is to be promoted.' Although the first American tariff (1789) levied only light duties on the importation of the most important manufactured articles, it yet worked so beneficially from the very first years of its introduction that Washington in his 'Message' in 1791 was able to congratulate the nation on the flourishing condition of its manufactures, agriculture, and trade.

The inadequacy of this protection was, however, soon apparent; for the effect of the slight import duties was easily overcome by English manufacturers, who had the advantage of improved methods of production. Congress did certainly raise the duty on the most important manufactured articles to fifteen per cent, but this was not till the year 1804, when it was compelled, owing to deficient customs receipts, to raise more revenue, and long after the inland manufacturers had exhausted every argument in favour of having more protection, while the interests opposed to them were equally strenuous upon the advantages of free trade and the injurious effects of high import duties.

In striking contrast with the slight progress which had, on the whole, been made by the manufacturers of the country, stood the improved condition of its navigation, which since the year 1789, upon the motion of James Madison, had received effectual protection. From a tonnage of 200,000 in 1789 their mercantile marine had increased in 1801 to more than 1,000,000 tons. Under the protection of the tariff of 1804, the manufacturing interest of the United States could just barely maintain itself against the English manufactories, which were continually being improved, and had attained a colossal magnitude, and it would doubtless have had to succumb entirely to English competition, had it not been for the help of the embargo and declaration of war of 1812. In consequence of these events, just as at the time of the War of Independence, the American manufactories received such an extraordinary impetus that they not only sufficed for the home demand, but soon began to export as well. According to a report of the Committee on Trade and Manufactures to Congress in 1815, 100,000 hands were employed in the woollen and cotton manufactures alone, whose yearly production amounted to the value of more than sixty million dollars. As in the days of the War of Independence, and as a necessary consequence of the increase in manufacturing power, there occurred a rapid rise in all prices, not only of produce and in wages, but also of landed property, and hence universal prosperity amongst landowners, labourers, and all engaged in internal trade.

After the peace of Ghent, Congress, warned by the experience of 1786, decreed that for the first year the previous duties should be doubled, and during this period the country continued to prosper. Coerced, however, by powerful private interests which were opposed to those of the manufacturers, and persuaded by the arguments of theorists, it resolved in the year 1816 to make a considerable reduction in the import duties, whereupon the same effects of external competition reappeared which had been experienced from 1786 to 1789, viz. ruin of manufactories, unsaleability of produce, fall in the value of property and general calamity among landowners. After the country had for a second time enjoyed in war time the blessings of peace, it suffered, for a second time, greater evils through peace than the most devastating war could have brought upon it. It was only in the year 1824, after the effects of the English corn laws had been made manifest to the full extent of their unwise tendency thus compelling the agricultural interest of the central, northern, and western states to make common cause with the manufacturing interest, that a somewhat higher tariff was passed in Congress, which, however, as Mr Huskisson immediately brought forward counteracting measures with the view of paralysing the effects of this tariff on English competition, soon proved insufficient, and had to be supplemented by the tariff of 1828, carried through Congress after a violent struggle.

Recently published official statistics(1*) of Massachusetts give a tolerable idea of the start taken by the manufactures of the United States, especially in the central and northern states of the Union, in consequence of the protective system, and in spite of the subsequent modification of the tariff of 1828. In the year 1837, there were in this State (Massachusetts) 282 cotton mills and 565,031 spindles in operation, employing 4,997 male and 14,757 female hands; 37,275,917 pounds of cotton were worked up, and 126,000,000 yards of textile fabrics manufactured, of the value of 13,056,659 dollars, produced by a capital of 14,369,719 dollars.

In the woollen manufacture there were 192 mills, 501 machines, and 3,612 male and 3,485 female operatives employed, who worked up 10,858,988 pounds of wool, and produced 11,313,426 yards of cloth, of the value of 10,399,807 dollars on a working capital of 5,770,750 dollars.   16,689,877 pairs of shoes and boots were manufactured (large quantities of shoes being exported to the western states), to the value of 14,642,520 dollars.

The other branches of manufacture stood in relative proportion to the above.

The combined value of the manufactures of the State (deducting shipbuilding) amounted to over 86 million dollars, with a working capital of about 60 million dollars.

The number of operatives (men) was 117,352; and the total number of inhabitants of the State (in 1837) was 701,331.

Misery, brutality, and crime are unknown among the manufacturing population here. On the contrary, among the numerous male and female factory workers the strictest morality, cleanliness, and neatness in dress, exist; libraries are established to furnish them with useful and instructive books; the work is not exhausting, the food nourishing and good. Most of the women save a dowry for themselves.(2*)

This last is evidently the effect of the cheap prices of the common necessaries of life, light taxation, and an equitable customs tariff. Let England repeal the restrictions on the import of agricultural produce, decrease the existing taxes on consumption by one-half or two-thirds, cover the loss by an income tax, and her factory workers will be put into the same position.

No nation has been so misconstrued and so misjudged as respects its future destiny and its national economy as the United States of North America, by theorists as well as by practical men. Adam Smith and J. B. Say had laid it down that the United States were, 'like Poland,' destined for agriculture. This comparison was not very flattering for the union of some dozen of new, aspiring, youthful republics, and the prospect thus held out to them for the future not very encouraging. The above-mentioned theorists had demonstrated that Nature herself had singled out the people of the United States exclusively for agriculture, so long as the richest arable land was to be had in their country for a mere trifle. Great was the commendation which had been bestowed upon them for so willingly acquiescing in Nature's ordinances, and thus supplying theorists with a beautiful example of the splendid working of the principle of free trade. The school, however, soon had to experience the mortification of losing this cogent proof of the correctness and applicability of their theories in practice, and had to endure the spectacle of the United States seeking their nation's welfare in a direction exactly opposed to that of absolute freedom of trade.

As this youthful nation had previously been the very apple of the eye of the schoolmen, so she now became the object of the heaviest condemnation on the part of the theorists of every nation in Europe. It was said to be a proof of the slight progress of the New World in political knowledge, that while the European nations were striving with the most honest zeal to render universal free trade possible, while England and France especially were actually engaged in endeavouring to make important advances towards this great philanthropic object, the United States of North America were seeking to promote their national prosperity by a return to that long-exploded mercantile system which had been clearly refuted by theory. A country like the United States, in which such measureless tracts of fruitful land still remained uncultivated and where wages ruled so high, could not utilise its material wealth and increase of population to better purpose than in agriculture; and when this should have reached complete development, then manufactures would arise in the natural course of events without artificial forcing. But by an artificial development of manufactures the United States would injure not only the countries which had long before enjoyed civilisation, but themselves most of all.

With the Americans, however, sound common sense, and the instinct of what was necessary for the nation, were more potent than a belief in theoretical propositions. The arguments of the theorists were thoroughly investigated, and strong doubts entertained of the infallibility of a doctrine which its own disciples were not willing to put in practice.

To the argument concerning the still uncultivated tracts of fruitful land, it was answered that tracts of such land in the populous, well-cultivated states of the Union which were ripe for manufacturing industry, were as rare as in Great Britain; that the surplus population of those states would have to migrate at great expense to the west, in order to bring tracts of land of that description into cultivation, thus not only annually causing the eastern states large losses in material and intellectual resources, but also, inasmuch as such emigration would transform customers into competitors, the value of landed property and agricultural produce would thereby be lessened. It could not be to the advantage of the Union that all waste land

124

belonging to it should be cultivated up to the Pacific Ocean before either the population, the civilisation, or the military power of the old states had been fully developed. On the contrary, the cultivation of distant virgin lands could confer no benefit on the eastern states unless they themselves devoted their attention to manufacturing, and could exchange their manufactures against the produce of the west. People went still further: Was not England, it was asked, in much the same position? Had not England also under her dominion vast tracts of fertile land still uncultivated in Canada, in Australia, and in other quarters of the world? Was it not almost as easy for England to transplant her surplus population to those countries as for the North Americans to transplant theirs from the shores of the Atlantic to the banks of the Missouri? If so, what occasion had England not only continuously to protect her home manufactures, but to strive to extend them more and more?

The argument of the school, that with a high rate of wages in agriculture, manufactures could not succeed by the natural course of things, but only by being forced like hothouse plants, was found to be partially well-founded; that is to say, it was applicable only to those manufactured goods which, being small in bulk and weight as compared to their value, are produced principally by hand labour, but was not applicable to goods the price of which is less influenced by the rate of wages, and as to which the disadvantage of higher wages can be neutralised by the use of machinery, by water power as yet unused, by cheap raw materials and food, by abundance of cheap fuel and building materials, by light taxation and increased efficiency of labour.

Besides, the Americans had long ago learnt from experience that agriculture cannot rise to a high state of prosperity unless the exchange of agricultural produce for manufactures is guaranteed for all future time; but that, when the agriculturist lives in America and the manufacturer in England, that exchange is not unfrequently interrupted by wars, commercial crises, or foreign tariffs, and that consequently, if the national well-being is to rest on a secure foundation, 'the manufacturer,' to use Jefferson's words, 'must come and settle down in close proximity to the agriculturist.'

At length the Americans came to realise the truth that it behoves a great nation not exclusively to set its heart upon the enjoyment of proximate material advantages; that civilisation and power — more important and desirable possessions than mere material wealth, as Adam Smith himself allows — can only be secured and retained by the creation of a manufacturing power of its own; that a country which feels qualified to take and to maintain its place amongst the powerful and civilised nations of the earth must not shrink from any sacrifice in order to secure such possessions for itself; and that at that time the Atlantic states were clearly the region marked out for such possessions.

It was on the shores of the Atlantic that European settlers and European civilisation first set a firm foot. Here, at the first, were populous, wealthy, and civilised states created; here was the cradle and seat of their sea fisheries, coasting trade, and naval power; here their independence was won and their union founded. Through these states on the coast the foreign trade of the Union is carried on; through them it is connected with the civilised world; through them it acquires the surplus population, material, capital, and mental powers of Europe; upon the civilisation, power, and wealth of these sea-board states depend the future civilisation, power, wealth, and independence of the whole nation and its future influence over less civilised communities. Suppose that the population of these Atlantic states

126

decreased instead of growing larger, that their fisheries, coasting trade, shipping engaged in foreign trade and foreign trade itself, and, above all, their general prosperity, were to fall off or remain stationary instead of progressing, then we should see the resources of civilisation of the whole nation, the guarantees for its independence and external power, diminish too in the same degree. It is even conceivable that, were the whole territory of the United States laid under cultivation from sea to sea, covered with agricultural states, and densely populated in the interior, the nation itself might nevertheless be left in a low grade as respects civilisation, independence, foreign power, and foreign trade. There are certainly many nationalities who are in such a position and whose shipping and naval power are nil, though possessing a numerous inland population!

If a power existed that cherished the project of keeping down the rise of the American people and bringing them under subjection to itself industrially, commercially, or politically, it could only succeed in its aim by trying to depopulate the Atlantic states of the Union and driving all increase of population, capital, and intellectual power into the interior. By that means it would not only check the further growth of the nation's naval power, but might also indulge the hope of getting possession in time of the principal defensive strategical positions on the Atlantic coast and at the mouths of the rivers. The means to this end would not be difficult to imagine; it would only be necessary to hinder the development of manufacturing power in the Atlantic states and to insure the acceptance of the principle of absolute freedom of foreign trade in America. If the Atlantic states do not become manufacturers, they will not only be unable to keep up their present degree of civilisation, but they must sink, and sink in every respect. Without manufactures how are the towns along the Atlantic coast to prosper?

Not by the forwarding of inland produce to Europe and of English manufactured goods to the interior, for a very few thousand people would be sufficient to transact this business. How are the fisheries to prosper? The majority of the population who have moved inland prefer fresh meat and fresh-water fish to salted; they require no train oil, or at least but a small quantity. How is the coasting trade along the Atlantic sea-board to thrive? As the largest portion of the coast states are peopled by cultivators of land who produce for themselves all the provisions, building materials, fuel, &c. which they require, there is nothing along the coast to sustain a transport trade. How are foreign trade and shipping to distant places to increase? The country has nothing to offer but what less cultivated nations possess in superabundance, and those manufacturing nations to which it sends its produce encourage their own shipping. How can a naval power arise when fisheries, the coasting trade, ocean navigation, and foreign trade decay? How are the Atlantic states to protect them selves against foreign attacks without a naval power? How is agriculture even to thrive in these states, when by means of canals, railways, &c. the produce of the much more fertile and cheaper tracts of land in the west which require no manure, can be carried to the east much more cheaply than it could be there produced upon soil exhausted long ago? How under such circumstances can civilisation thrive and population increase in the eastern states, when it is clear that under free trade with England all increase of population and of agricultural capital must flow to the west? The present state of Virginia gives but a faint idea of the condition into which the Atlantic states would be thrown by the absence of manufactures in the east; for Virginia, like all the southern states on the Atlantic coast, at present takes a profitable share in providing the Atlantic states with agricultural

128

produce.

All these things bear quite a different complexion, owing to the existence of a flourishing manufacturing power in the Atlantic states. Now population, capital, technical skill and intellectual power, flow into them from all European countries; now the demand for the manufactured products of the Atlantic states increases simultaneously with their consumption of the raw materials supplied by the west. Now the population of these states, their wealth, and the number and extent of their towns increase in equal proportion with the cultivation of the western virgin lands; now, on account of the larger population, and the consequently increased demand for meat, butter, cheese, milk, garden produce, oleaginous seeds, fruit, &c., their own agriculture is increasing; now the sea fisheries are flourishing in consequence of the larger demand for salted fish and train oil; now quantities of provisions, building materials, coal, &c. are being conveyed along the coast to furnish the wants of the manufacturing population; now the manufacturing population produce a large quantity of commodities for export to all the nations of the earth, from whence result profitable return freights; now the nation's naval power increases by means of the coasting trade, the fisheries, and navigation to distant lands, and with it the guarantee of national independence and influence over other nations, particularly over those of South America; now science and art, civilisation and literature, are improving in the eastern states, whence they are being diffused amongst the western states.

These were the circumstances which induced the United States to lay restrictions upon the importation of foreign manufactured goods, and to protect their native manufactures. With what amount of success this has been done, we have shown in the preceding pages. That without such a policy a manufacturing power could never have been maintained successfully in the Atlantic states, we may learn from their own experience and from the industrial history of other nations.

The frequently recurring commercial crises in America have been very often attributed to these restrictions on importation of foreign goods, but without reasonable grounds. The earlier as well as the later experience of North America shows, on the contrary, that such crises have never been more frequent and destructive than when commercial intercourse with England was least subject to restrictions. Commercial crises amongst agricultural nations, who procure their supplies of manufactured goods from foreign markets, arise from the disproportion between imports and exports. Manufacturing nations richer in capital than agricultural states, and ever anxious to increase the quantity of their exports, deliver their goods on credit and encourage consumption. In fact, they make advances upon the coming harvest. But if the harvest turn out so poor that its value falls greatly below that of the goods previously consumed; or if the harvest prove so rich that the supply of produce meets with no adequate demand and falls in price; while at the same time the markets still continue to be overstocked with foreign goods — then a commercial crisis will occur by reason of the disproportion existing between the means of payment and the quantity of goods previously consumed, as also by reason of the disproportion between supply and demand in the markets for produce and manufactured goods. The operations of foreign and native banks may increase and promote such a crisis, but they cannot create it. In a future chapter we shall endeavour more closely to elucidatc this subject.

NOTES:

1. Statistical Table of Massachusetts for the Year ending April 1, 1837, by J. P. Bigelow, Secretary of the Commonwealth (Boston, 1838). No American state but Massachusetts possesses similar statistical abstracts. We owe those here referred to, to Governor Everett, distinguished alike as a scholar, an author, and a statesman.

2. The American papers of July 1839 report that in the manufacturing town of Lowell alone there are over a hundred workwomen who have each over a thousand dollars deposited to their credit in the savings bank.

Chapter 10

The Teachings of History

Everywhere and at all times has the well-being of the nation been in equal proportion to the intelligence, morality, and industry of its citizens; according to these, wealth has accrued or been diminished; but industry and thrift, invention and enterprise, on the part of individuals, have never as yet accomplished aught of importance where they were not sustained by municipal liberty, by suitable public institutions and laws, by the State administration and foreign policy, but above all by the unity and power, of the nation.

History everywhere shows us a powerful process of reciprocal action between the social and the individual powers and conditions. In the Italian and the Hanseatic cities, in Holland and England, in France and America, we find the powers of production, and consequently the wealth of individuals, growing in proportion to the liberties enjoyed, to the degree of perfection of political and social institutions, while these, on the other hand, derive material and stimulus for their further improvement from the increase of the material wealth and of the productive power of individuals.

The real rise of the industry and power of England dates only from the days of the actual foundation of England's national freedom, while the industry and power of Venice, of the Hanse Towns, of the Spanish and Portuguese, decayed concurrently with their loss of freedom. However industrious, thrifty, inventive, and intelligent, individual citizens might be, they could not make up for the lack of free institutions. History also teaches that individuals derive the greater part of their productive powers from the social institutions and conditions under which they are placed.

The influence of liberty, intelligence, and enlightenment over the power, and therefore over the productive capacity and wealth of a nation, is exemplified in no respect so clearly as in navigation. Of all industrial pursuits, navigation most demands energy, personal courage, enterprise, and endurance; qualifications that can only flourish in an atmosphere of freedom. In no other calling do ignorance, superstition, and prejudice, indolence, cowardice, effeminacy, and weakness produce such disastrous consequences; nowhere else is a sense of self-reliance so indispensable. Hence history cannot point to a single example of an enslaved people taking a prominent part in navigation. The Hindoos, the Chinese, and the Japanese have ever strictly confined their efforts to canal and river navigation and the coasting trade. In ancient Egypt maritime navigation was held in abhorrence, probably because priests and rulers dreaded lest by means of it the spirit of freedom and independence should be encouraged. The freest and most enlightened states of ancient Greece were also the most powerful at sea; their naval power ceased with their freedom, and however much history may narrate of the victories of the kings of Macedonia on land, she is silent as to their victories at sea.

When were the Romans powerful at sea, and when is nothing more heard of their fleets? When did Italy lay down the law in the Mediterranean, and since when has her very coasting trade fallen into the hands of foreigners? Upon the Spanish navy the Inquisition had passed sentence of death long ere the English and the Dutch fleets had executed the decree. With the coming into power of the mercantile oligarchies in the Hanse Towns, power and the spirit of enterprise took leave of the Hanseatic

League.

Of the Spanish Netherlands only the maritime provinces achieved their freedom, whereas those held in subjection by the Inquisition had even to submit to the closing of their rivers. The English fleet, victorious over the Dutch in the Channel, now took possession of the dominion of the seas, which the spirit of freedom had assigned to England long before; and yet Holland, down to our own days, has retained a large proportion of her mercantile marine, whereas that of the Spaniards and the Portuguese is almost annihilated. In vain were the efforts of a great individual minister now and then under the despotic kings of France to create a fleet, for it invariably went again to ruin.

But how is it that at the present day we witness the growing strength of French navigation and naval power? Hardly had the independence of the United States of North America come to life, when we find the Americans contending with renown against the giant fleets of the mother country. But what is the position of the Central and South American nations? So long as their flags wave not over every sea, but little dependence can be placed upon the effectiveness of their republican forms of government. Contrast these with Texas, a territory that has scarcely attained to political life, and yet already claims its share in the realm of Neptune.

But navigation is merely one part of the industrial power of a nation — a part which can flourish and attain to importance only in conjunction with all the other complementary parts. Everywhere and at all times we see navigation, inland and foreign trade, and even agriculture itself, flourish only where manufactures have reached a high state of prosperity. But if freedom be an indispensable condition for the prosperity of navigation, how much wore must it be so for the prosperity of the manufacturing power, for the growth of the entire producing power of a nation? History contains no record of a rich, commercial, and industrial community that was not at the same time in the enjoyment of freedom.

Manufactures everywhere first brought into operation improved weans of transport, improved river navigation, improved highways, steam navigation and railways, which constitute the fundamental elements of improved systems of agriculture and of civilisation.

History teaches that arts and trades migrated from city to city, from one country to another. Persecuted and oppressed at home, they took refuge in cities and in countries where freedom, protection, and support were assured to them. In this way they migrated from Greece and Asia to Italy; from Italy to Germany, Flanders, and Brabant; and from thence to Holland and England. Everywhere it was want of sense and despotism that drove them away, and the spirit of freedom that attracted them. But for the folly of the Continental governments, England would have had difficulty in attaining supremacy in industry. But does it appear more consistent with wisdom for us in Germany to wait patiently until other nations are impolitic enough to drive out their industries and thus compel them to seek a refuge with us, or that we should, without waiting for such contingencies, invite them by proffered advantages to settle down amongst us?

It is true that experience teaches that the wind bears the seed from one region to another, and that thus waste moorlands have been transformed into dense forests; but would it on that account be wise policy for the forester to wait until the wind in the course of ages effects this transformation?

Is it unwise on his part if by sowing and planting he seeks to attain the same object within a few decades? History tells us that whole nations have successfully accomplished that which we see the forester do? Single free cities, or small republics and confederations of such cities and states, limited in territorial possessions, of small population and insignificant military power, but fortified by the energy of youthful freedom and favoured by geographical position as well as by fortunate circumstances and opportunities, flourished by means of manufactures and commerce long before the great monarchies; and by free commercial intercourse with the latter, by which they exported to them manufactured goods and imported raw produce in exchange, raised themselves to a high degree of wealth and power. Thus did Venice, the Hanse Towns the Belgians and the Dutch.

Nor was this system of free trade less profitable at first to the great monarchies themselves, with whom these smaller communities had commercial intercourse. For, having regard to the wealth of their natural resources and to their undeveloped social condition the free importation of foreign manufactured goods and the exportation of native produce presented the surest and most effectual means of developing their own powers of production, of instilling habits of industry into their subjects who were addicted to idleness and turbulence, of inducing their landowners and nobles to feel an interest in industry, of arousing the dormant spirit of enterprise amongst their merchants, and especially of raising their own civilisation, industry, and power.

These effects were learned generally by Great Britain from the trade and manufacturing industry of the Italians, the Hansards, the Belgians, and the Dutch. But having attained to a certain grade of development by means of free trade, the great monarchies perceived that the highest degree of civilisation, power, and wealth can only be attained by a combination of manufactures and commerce with agriculture. They perceived that their newly established native manufactures could never hope to succeed in free competition with the old and long established manufactures of foreigners; that their native fisheries and native mercantile marine, the foundations of their naval power, could never make successful progress without special privileges; and that the spirit of enterprise of their native merchants would always be kept down by the overwhelming reserves of capital, the greater experience and sagacity of the foreigners. Hence they sought, by a system of restrictions, privileges, and encouragements, to transplant on to their native soil the wealth, the talents, and the spirit of enterprise of the foreigners. This policy was pursued with greater or lesser, with speedier or more tardy success, just in proportion as the measures adopted were more or less judiciously adapted to the object in view, and applied and pursued with more or less energy and perseverance.

England, above all other nations, has adopted this policy. Often interrupted in its execution from the want of intelligence and self-restraint on the part of her rulers, or owing to internal commotions and foreign wars, it first assumed the character of a settled and practically efficient policy under Edward VI, Elizabeth, and the revolutionary period. For how could the measures of Edward III work satisfactorily when it was not till under Henry VI that the law permitted the carriage of corn from one English county to another, or the shipment of it to foreign parts; when still under Henry VII and Henry VIII all interest on money, even discount on bills, was held to be usury, and when it was still thought at the time that trade might be encouraged by fixing by law at a low figure the price of woollen goods and the rate of wages, and that the production of corn could be increased by prohibiting sheep farming on a large scale?

And how much sooner would England's woollen manufac-

137

tures and maritime trade have reached a high standard of prosperity had not Henry VIII regarded a rise in the prices of corn as an evil; had he, instead of driving foreign workmen by wholesale from the kingdom, sought like his predecessors to augment their number by encouraging their immigration; and had not Henry VII refused his sanction to the Act of Navigation as proposed by Parliament?

In France we see native manufactures, free internal intercourse, foreign trade, fisheries, navigation, and naval power — in a word, all the attributes of a great, mighty, and rich nation (which it had cost England the persevering efforts of centuries to acquire) — called into existence by a great genius within the space of a few years, as it were by a magician's wand; and afterwards all of them yet more speedily annihilated by the iron hand of fanaticism and despotism.

We see the principle of free trade contending in vain under unfavourable conditions against restriction powerfully enforced; the Hanseatic League is ruined, while Holland sinks under the blows of England and France.

That a restrictive commercial policy can be operative for good only so far as it is supported by the progressive civilisation and free institutions of a nation, we learn from the decay of Venice, Spain, and Portugal, from the relapse of France in consequence of the revocation of the Edict of Nantes, and from the history of England, in which country liberty kept pace at all times with the advance of industry, trade, and national wealth.

That, on the contrary, a highly advanced state of civilisation, with or without free institutions, unless supported by a suitable system of commercial policy, will prove but a poor guarantee for a nation's economic progress, may be learnt on the one hand from the history of the North American free states, and on

138

the other from the experience of Germany.

Modern Germany, lacking a system of vigorous and united commercial policy, exposed in her home markets to competition with a foreign manufacturing power in every way superior to her own, while excluded at the same time from foreign markets by arbitrary and often capricious restrictions, and very far indeed from making that progress in industry to which her degree of culture entitles her, cannot even maintain her previously acquired position, and is made a convenience of (like a colony) by that very nation which centuries ago was worked upon in like manner by the merchants of Germany, until at last the German states have resolved to secure their home markets for their own industry, by the adoption of a united vigorous system of commercial policy.

The North American free states, who, more than any other nation before them, are in a position to benefit by freedom of trade, and influenced even from the very cradle of their independence by the doctrines of the cosmopolitan school, are striving more than any other nation to act on that principle. But owing to wars with Great Britain, we find that nation twice compelled to manufacture at home the goods which it previously purchased under free trade from other countries, and twice, after the conclusion of peace, brought to the brink of ruin by free competition with foreigners, and thereby admonished of the fact that under the present conditions of the world every great nation must seek the guarantees of its continued prosperity and independence, before all other things, in the independent and uniform development of its own powers and resources.

Thus history shows that restrictions are not so much the inventions of mere speculative minds, as the natural consequences of the diversity of interests, and of the strivings of nations after independence or overpowering ascendency, and thus of national emulation and wars, and therefore that they cannot be dispensed with until this conflict of national interests shall cease, in other words until all nations can be united under one and the same system of law. Thus the question as to whether, and how, the various nations can be brought into one united federation, and how the decisions of law can be invoked in the place of military force to determine the differences which arise between independent nations, has to be solved concurrently with the question how universal free trade can be established in the place of separate national commercial systems.

The attempts which have been made by single nations to introduce freedom of trade in face of a nation which is predominant in industry, wealth, and power, no less than distinguished for an exclusive tariff system — as Portugal did in 1703, France in 1786, North America in 1786 and 1816, Russia from 1815 till 1821, and as Germany has done for centuries — go to show us that in this way the prosperity of individual nations is sacrificed, without benefit to mankind in general, solely for the enrichment of the predominant manufacturing and commercial nation. Switzerland (as we hope to show in the sequel) constitutes an exception, which proves just as much as it proves little for or against one or the other system.

Colbert appears to us not to have been the inventor of that system which the Italians have named after him; for, as we have seen, it was fully elaborated by the English long before his time. Colbert only put in practice what France, if she wished to fulfil her destinies, was bound to carry out sooner or later. If Colbert is to be blamed at all, it can only be charged against him that he attempted to put into force under a despotic government a system which could subsist only after a fundamental reform of the political conditions. But against this reproach to Colbert's memory it may very well be argued that, had his system been continued by wise princes and sagacious ministers, it would in all probability have removed by means of reforms all those hindrances which stood in the way of progress in manufactures, agriculture, and trade, as well as of national freedom; and France would then have undergone no revolution, but rather, impelled along the path of development by the reciprocating influences of industry and freedom, she might for the last century and a half have been successfully competing with England in manufactures, in the promotion of her internal trade, in foreign commerce, and in colonisation, as well as in her fisheries, her navigation, and her naval power.

Finally, history teaches us how nations which have been endowed by Nature with all resources which are requisite for the attainment of the highest grade of wealth and power, may and must — without on that account forfeiting the end in view — modify their systems according to the measure of their own progress: in the first stage, adopting free trade with more advanced nations as a means of raising themselves from a state of barbarism, and of making advances in agriculture; in the second stage, promoting the growth of manufactures, fisheries, navigation, and foreign trade by means of commercial restrictions; and in the last stage, after reaching the highest degree of wealth and power, by gradually reverting to the principle of free trade and of unrestricted competition in the home as well as in foreign markets, that so their agriculturists, manufacturers, and merchants may be preserved from indolence, and stimulated to retain the supremacy which they have acquired. In the first stage, we see Spain, Portugal, and the Kingdom of Naples; in the second, Germany and the United States of North America; France apparently stands close upon the boundary line of the last stage; but Great Britain alone at the present time has actually reached it.

COSIMO is an innovative publisher of books and publications that inspire, inform and engage readers worldwide. Our titles are drawn from a range of subjects including health, business, philosophy, history, science and sacred texts. We specialize in using print-on-demand technology (POD), making it possible to publish books for both general and specialized audiences and to keep books in print indefinitely. With POD technology new titles can reach their audiences faster and more efficiently than with traditional publishing.

> ➢ **Permanent Availability:** Our books & publications never go out-of-print.

> ➢ **Global Availability:** Our books are always available online at popular retailers and can be ordered from your favorite local bookstore.

COSIMO CLASSICS brings to life unique, rare, out-of-print classics representing subjects as diverse as *Alternative Health, Business and Economics, Eastern Philosophy, Personal Growth, Mythology, Philosophy, Sacred Texts, Science, Spirituality* and much more!

COSIMO-on-DEMAND publishes your books, publications and reports. If you are an Author, part of an Organization, or a Benefactor with a publishing project and would like to bring books back into print, publish new books fast and effectively, would like your publications, books, training guides, and conference reports to be made available to your members and wider audiences around the world, we can assist you with your publishing needs.

Visit our website at www.cosimobooks.com to learn more about Cosimo, browse our catalog, take part in surveys or campaigns, and sign-up for our newsletter.

And if you wish please drop us a line at info@cosimobooks.com. We look forward to hearing from you.

Printed in the United Kingdom by
Lightning Source UK Ltd., Milton Keynes
139070UK00001B/34/A